Simcha's Torah Stories

Simcha's Torah Stories

Rabbi Simcha Groffman

TARGUM/FELDHEIM

First published 2000
Copyright © 2000 by Simcha Groffman
ISBN 1-56871-119-0

Published by:
Targum Press, Inc.
22700 W. Eleven Mile Rd.
Southfield, MI 48034
E-mail: targum@elronet.co.il
Fax toll free: 888-298-9992

Distributed by:
Feldheim Publishers
200 Airport Executive Park
Nanuet, NY 10954
www.feldheim.com

Printed in Israel

Acknowledgements

With praise and gratitude to Hashem Yisborach, I wish to thank those who assisted me in the writing and publishing of this book.

- To Rabbi Sholom Eisemann, for his guidance in the field of *chinuch banim* and *divrei Torah* for children.

- To Rabbi Mendel Weinbach, for sharing his wealth of wisdom and experience in writing and other areas. He and Rabbi Moshe Newman employed me to write children's stories and have allowed them to be reprinted in this book.

- To the staff of Targum Press, whose expertise and professionalism make book publishing a pleasure.

- To the readers of "Kinder Torah," my weekly *parashah* sheet, for giving me the opportunity to spread Torah every week.

- To the Glassman, Chernick, and Schwartz families, for their kind support.

- To my cousins, Mr. and Mrs. Melvin Steinig, for their thoughtfulness.

- To my mother-in-law, Mrs. Malka Shafer, whose presence has added immeasurably to the *ruchnius* of our Shabbos table and who has encouraged me in all of my writing.

- To my brother Aaron and his family, for their support and encouragement.

- To my parents, Mr. and Mrs. Robert Groffman, whose main goal in life has been the education of their children. With common sense, warmth, and sensitivity, they taught me, by personal example, the paramount importance of a close relationship between parents and children.

- To my *kinderlach*, Ahuva Bayla, Leah, Devorah Esther, and Shoshana Raizel, who help me every day to be a better Tattie than I was the day before.

- Lastly, to my wife Sara, whose *mesiras nefesh* for my Torah learning and the education of our children is a continual source of *berachah* in our lives. This book and indeed all of my accomplishments are in her merit. "Her husband's heart trusts in her, and he lacks no fortune."

*This book is dedicated
in loving memory of*

Mr. and Mrs. Stanley Weiner
Mr. Victor Groffman
Mr. and Mrs. Elimelech Lenzner
Mr. and Mrs. Yaakov Eli Rosenblatt
Shmuel Ben Zion Yosef Lenzner
Zahava Lurie
Hillel and Rene Libauer
Boris Glassman
Leib ben Dovid
Mr. and Mrs. Nathan Schwartz
Samuel B. Schwartz
Scott Barry Weiner
Mirele bas Leah
Yitzchak Dovid ben Shmuel Yosef
Mordechai Dovid ben Avigdor
Aryeh Leib ben Yerachmiel
Yerachmiel ben Leizer

Bereishis

Parashas Bereishis

It Keeps the World Running

Chaim, wake up! You don't want to oversleep today. To-day is your big class trip."

"*Oy vey*, Mommy! What time is it? Am I late?"

"No, Chaim, you still have time. But don't delay."

"I'm so excited, Mommy. Today we are going to see the electric company's big power plant."

"It sounds great, Chaim. Have a great time. And tell us all about it."

"Wow, look at that, Avi! A huge generator. It must be as big as a four-story building — and half a city block long. I have a question to ask our tour guide, the chief engineer."

"There he is, Chaim. You can ask him now."

"Excuse me, sir, but what makes this huge generator run?"

"That's a very good question, young man. This hydro-dynamic generator is fueled by the combustion of liquid pe-troleum fuel oil."

"Do you mean, sir, that fuel oil contains enough energy

to run this huge generator?"

"Yes, that is correct, young man."

"Excuse me, sir, but where does the fuel oil get the energy?"

"Young man, you have asked another good question. According to current theories, fossil fuels get their energy from the decay of organic matter."

"Wow, organic matter. What's that?"

"Trees, plants, and even animals that have died and become buried deep in the earth."

"I am sorry to ask so many questions, sir, but where did the plants and animals get the energy from?"

"What is your name, young man?"

"My name is Chaim, sir."

"Chaim, all energy on the earth ultimately comes from the sun. The sunlight is captured by living things and stored as energy within them."

"Where does the sun get its energy from?"

"Chaim, the sun generates energy with nuclear fission and fusion. Atoms and molecules are broken down at their simplest levels to generate huge amounts of energy."

"And where do the atoms get their energy, sir?"

"Chaim, we've had enough questions for now. It's time to continue with the tour."

"Well, Chaim, how was your tour of the power plant today?"

"Great, Daddy. We saw a huge generator, and I asked the chief engineer all kinds of questions. There was only one question that he didn't answer."

"What was that, Chaim?"

"Where do atoms get their energy from?"

"Chaim, we learn that from *parashas Bereishis*, the very first *parashah* in the Torah. Hashem created the Torah before He created the world. The Torah is the blueprint for the world. Hashem used the blueprint to create the world. Why did Hashem create the world? For the Jewish people to learn Torah. Besides the Torah being the blueprint of the world, it provides the energy that keeps this world running."

"Really, Daddy? How is that?"

"Our Sages tell us that if for one moment all Torah learning would cease, the world would collapse. It would return to the nothingness that existed before creation. So you see, it is your Torah learning that provides the energy that keeps the atoms, the sun, the earth, the electric power station, and all of the world running."

"Daddy, I'd love to talk longer, but I had better get back to learning!"

"Chaim, you're the greatest."

Simcha's Brain Teaser

If today is Monday, what is the day after the day before the day before tomorrow?

For the answer, turn to the back of the book.

They Didn't Take Him Seriously

N oach, what are you doing?"

"I am planting a tree."

"There are already so many beautiful trees in the world, why are you planting another one?"

"This is a special type of tree called gopher, whose wood is very light."

"Why do you need a tree with light wood, Noach?"

"I will use the wood to build a *teivah*."

"Why do you need a *teivah*? Who told you to build it?"

"Hashem commanded me to build it. If the people in the world continue to commit terrible sins, Hashem is going to bring a flood to destroy the whole world. Only those inside of the *teivah* will survive the flood."

"Noach, you are a nice man, but that story is a little far-fetched. We are very strong, powerful people. Nothing car destroy us. Neither flood, nor fire, nor wind. We can survive them all."

"If I were you, I would take this more seriously."

Fifty years later...

"Noach, your trees have really grown big and strong!"

"Yes, I am getting ready to cut them down now."

"You still haven't given up on your idea of building a teivah?"

"It is not my idea. Hashem told me to do it. I would strongly suggest that you examine your life and see if you are living according to Hashem's wishes. There will come a day when Hashem will send a flood to destroy the world."

"Have a nice day, Noach."

Fifty years later...

"Noach, what is that big thing you are building? It looks like the framework of a boat."

"That's exactly what it is. A big boat called a *teivah*."

"Oh, I remember you, your *teivah*, and your flood. You are really serious about this. What are you going to put into this *teivah*?"

"I am going to gather together two of every animal in the world, and seven of each of the kosher animals, and lead them into this *teivah*. Then I am going to put in enough food to feed them for a year."

"Ha ha! Your *teivah* isn't that big. You will need a *teivah* ten times that size to hold all of the animals in the world. Then you will need space for all of the food that they will eat. How will you find all of these animals? And once you find them, how are you going to gather them all up and get them here? Do you really think they can live together in this *teivah*? You are going to put lions together with sheep? When that lion gets hungry, you won't have any sheep left. You are going to put deer in that small place? Deer need space to run around. Noach, be realistic."

"Do you think that anything is too difficult for Hashem? He can line up all of the animals and fit them all, along with provisions, into this little *teivah*, easier than you can snap your fingers. Which is exactly what He will do if you do not do as He says. Return to Him while you still can."

"Noach, you have a good imagination."

Twenty years later...

"Noach, Noach! Let us into the *teivah*! The whole world is flooding!"

"I spoke to you many times over the past 120 years. I warned you over and over again that this would happen. You did not listen to me. Now it is too late..."

Simcha's Brain Teaser

Sisters and brothers have I none, but that man's father is my father's son. Who is that man?

For the answer, turn to the back of the book.

Tests

"Chaim, how did you do on the test today?"

"Pretty good, Avi. I think I only got one or two questions wrong. How did you do?"

"Not so good. I guess I didn't study well enough. These tests are hard."

"You're right, Avi, but that really makes us learn the subject well. After I study and do well on one of those tests, I really know my stuff."

"So true, Chaim. I guess I need some encouragement."

"I can help you with that, Avi. This week we learned about Avraham Avinu and the tests that he passed. Hashem was the One who tested him. His tests were different from ours. There is a similarity, however. Both tests were given to help the one being tested. Our tests help us study better. Avraham's tests helped him grow closer to Hashem."

"Can you give me an example of one of Avraham Avinu's tests, Chaim?"

"Sure, Avi. *Lech Lecha*."

"Isn't that the name of this week's *parashah*?"

"Yes it is. Hashem told Avraham to leave his homeland to go live in a new country."

"What's so hard about that, Chaim? I hear about people moving cross-country or even overseas all of the time."

"Things were a little different then, Avi. There were no jet planes to make travel quick and easy. Avraham Avinu had to travel by horse and wagon. It took weeks or even months to reach the destination. The roads were rough, and bandits attacked the travelers. Food was also a problem. Even after the traveler arrived and settled into his new home, it was not easy. He was in a strange place and had to adjust to a new life: new faces, a new language, new customs. The hardest part was being cut off from his loved ones. There were no telephones, fax machines, or e-mail to connect far-

away places. When a person left his homeland, he would probably never see or communicate with his family and friends again."

"That's such a hard test."

"You're right, Avi. That shows you how much Avraham Avinu loved Hashem. He passed the test and left his home-land. This was not the only test. There were nine others. Avraham Avinu passed them all."

"Wow!"

"*Pirkei Avos* says that Hashem had a great love for Avraham Avinu because he passed all of the tests. I hope this inspires you to do well on your tests, Avi. Just remember that tests are given to us for our own good."

"Thanks so much, Chaim. You've really passed the test of helping a friend in need."

Simcha's Brain Teaser

A shepherd had one sheep behind two sheep, one sheep in front of two sheep, and one sheep between two sheep. How many sheep did he have altogether?

For the answer, turn to the back of the book.

Don't Mind the Aches and Pains

Shalom, Avi! How are you? You look like you're on your way to the pool."

"Right you are, Chaim. I'm just trying to stay cool in this hot weather. It must be 90° today."

"I'm very hot, too, Avi. I am so glad that I met you. I am on my way to do a big mitzvah."

"Great, Chaim! What is it?"

"Mr. Goodman, the elderly man who lives next door to me, is moving tomorrow. He is too old to live by himself, so he is moving near his daughter. He still has some packing left to do. There are books, clothes, and some dishes. I am trying to get some friends to come and help him put these things into boxes. What do you say, Avi?"

"Boy, it sure is hot today, Chaim. I am so tired. I couldn't sleep last night because of the heat. I think a nice relaxing day at the pool would suit me just fine."

"Avi, if you think it is hot today, let me tell you about another very hot day, a long, long time ago. Just imagine that you are Avraham Avinu, sitting in your tent in a place called Mamre..."

"It is very hot here today. I feel very weak. Only three days ago, I had my *bris milah*. I am in pain. I am ninety-nine years old, not a young man anymore. But nothing pains me as much as the fact that no guests are coming to visit me to-

day. I want very badly to do the mitzvah of entertaining guests in my home. Eliezer, will you please be so kind as to go out to see if any travelers are coming our way?"

A short time later, Eliezer returns without any guests.

"Perhaps Eliezer did not look carefully enough. I will go out and look myself...I don't see any guests...Wait a minute! I see three men coming! Weary travelers, please come this way. Stop here for a little refreshment. Please, my honored guests, take a little water. I will get some bread for you.

"Now that I am doing a mitzvah, I forgot all about my aches and pains and the hot weather. I must run to serve them the finest food and drink.

"Sarah, my dear wife, may I trouble you to please bake fresh bread for our guests? I am going to prepare for them the choicest meat delicacy. I want to give them a sumptuous meal, fit for a king."

"Chaim, you have such a nice way of pointing me in the right direction. I have a mitzvah to do! I feel cooler already."

Simcha's Brain Teaser

A certain family party consisted of one grandfather, one grandmother, two fathers, two mothers, four children, three grandchildren, one brother, two sisters, two sons, two daughters, one father-in-law, one mother-in-law, and one daughter-in-law. A total of twenty-three people, you might think. But, no! How many people were there? And how?

For the answer, turn to the back of the book.

Enough to Quench the Biggest Thirst

"Chaim, come look at the lions' cage! Over there is Monkey Island! Isn't the zoo great?"

"Avi, wait a few minutes while I stay here at the camels' cage."

"What's so interesting about camels?"

"I'm watching this camel drink. Do you see him? He's been drinking water for ten minutes. I want to see how long it takes to quench his thirst...

"Mr. Zookeeper, can you answer a question for us?"

"Sure, boys, what would you like to know?"

"How much water can a camel drink?"

"Camels have been known to drink up to forty gallons of water at one time."

"Forty gallons! How much is that?"

"The hot water tank in your home holds about forty gallons."

"Wow, that's a lot of water."

"Boys, that is why camels are excellent desert animals. When they fill up with water, they can travel long distances in the desert without drinking."

"Mr. Zookeeper, do you know that our ancestor Rivka drew enough well water to quench the thirst of ten camels?"

"Did she have an electric pump?"

"No, she lived in the days before electricity. She drew the water by hand. Our father Avraham sent his servant Eliezer to look for a young woman who would be a suitable wife for his son, Yitzchak."

"What were the criteria for a suitable wife for Yitzchak?"

"She had to be kindhearted in the same way as our father Avraham. When he saw a person in need, he ran to help him. He did much more than was asked for."

"What did Rivka do?"

"Eliezer, his men, and ten camels arrived from their journey at the end of the day. They went to the well and Eliezer asked Rivka for a little water to drink. She drew enough water from the well for him, his men, and his ten camels."

"Wow! If each camel could drink forty gallons, that could have been 400 gallons of water! It must have been quite a feat for one girl to draw all of that water by hand."

"Rivka was quite a young woman, overflowing with lovingkindness and concern for others."

"Look, Avi, the camel has finally stopped drinking. After seeing how much water he drinks, I have a new appreciation for our ancestor Rivka. She helped to build our nation with acts of lovingkindness. I hope that someday I can marry a girl like that."

"Chaim, I have no doubt that you will."

Simcha's Brain Teaser

Every day, a wife picks up her husband at the train station at five o'clock. One day he arrives early, at four o'clock, and he begins to walk home along the road on which his wife will be traveling. She meets him and takes him the rest of the way. If he would have waited at the train station, she would have arrived at five. As it turned out, they reached home 20 minutes early.

What time was it when she picked him up?

For the answer, turn to the back of the book.

Keep Plugging Away

O kay, Chaim, let's go over your multiplication tables."

"Great, Daddy."

"Four times three?"

"Twelve."

"Five times seven?"

"Thirty-five."

"Nine times six?"

"Fifty-two."

"Chaim, try again."

"Oh, Daddy. I'm so frustrated! I'm having such trouble with those nines. I'm never going to master these multiplication tables. *Oy vey.*"

"Chaim, let me tell you a true story about frustration. You know that in the old days, people did not have water faucets in their homes."

"Sure, Daddy. People used to go to the well to get water."

"Chaim, people even had to dig their own wells. That was very hard work, digging down deep for water. There were no power tools. Avraham Avinu dug many water wells. Unfortunately, when he left the land of Canaan, the Pelishtim took over and stopped up all of the wells. Yitzchak Avinu returned to the land and reopened the wells that Avraham had dug. Then he dug more wells. The local shepherds claimed the water was theirs and began to fight with Yitzchak's shepherds over the wells. Yitzchak left those wells and dug a new well. There was a fight over that well also, and Yitzchak again moved on and dug a new well. Finally, this well was not contested. He called this last well Rechovot."

"Wow, Daddy, Yitzchak Avinu sure had to dig a lot of wells."

"That's correct, Chaim. The great sage Rav Yisrael Meir Kagan, who is known to us as the Chafetz Chaim, learns an important lesson from this episode."

"What's that, Daddy?"

"A person does not always succeed the first time he tries something. He should not get frustrated and give up. We see how many times our father Yitzchak dug well after well after well, until he finally dug one that was not contested. He could have given up many times, but he did not. He kept plugging. We have many challenges in our lives. We may not succeed the first time. Nor the second time. Nor the third time. That is no reason to give up. The Chafetz Chaim encourages us to keep plugging. Try, and try again, until we succeed."

"Thanks so much, Daddy. That was great."

"Okay, Chaim. How much is nine times six?"

"Fifty-four."

"Right! Chaim, you're a real plugger."

Simcha's Brain Teaser

A rich old man has three sons. When he died, he willed his 17 camels to the sons, to be divided as follows: First son to get 1/2 of the camels, second son to get 1/3 of the camels, third son to get 1/9 of the camels. The sons are sitting there trying to figure out how this can possibly be done, when a very old, wise man goes riding by. They stop him and ask him to help them solve their problem. Without hesitation he divides the camels properly and continues riding on his way. How did he do it?

For the answer, turn to the back of the book.

Parashas Vayetzei

You Make the Difference

Avi, Avi, I'm so glad I ran into you today!"

"What's doing, Chaim?"

"First of all, how are you? How are you feeling?"

"Fine, Chaim. Thank you for asking. How are you?"

"Just fine, thank you. Avi, do you know that new neighbors just moved into the house down the street yesterday?"

"I thought I saw a moving truck there."

"Well, they need help with everything, as you can imagine. I got about fifteen guys together to help them this afternoon. Can you come?"

"Fifteen guys! Chaim you're a super organizer. Fifteen guys can do anything. It sounds like you don't even need me. What difference will I make?"

"Avi, everybody makes a difference. Your efforts are very important."

"How do you know that, Chaim?"

"We learn it from this week's Torah portion, *Vayetzei*. The Torah begins by telling us that Yaakov Avinu left the city of Be'er Sheva and traveled toward the city of Haran. Our

Sages ask the question: Why did the Torah tell us that Yaakov left Be'er Sheva? The Torah could have written that Yaakov went to the city of Haran, and we would have automatically known that he left Be'er Sheva."

"What is the answer to that question, Chaim?"

"The Torah is teaching us a lesson, Avi."

"What lesson is that?"

"When a righteous person such as Yaakov Avinu lives in a city, he has a very big positive influence on that city. He improves the whole quality of life there. When he leaves that city, the loss is felt. The Torah tells us that Yaakov left Be'er Sheva to teach us that his presence was missed there."

"That is a beautiful lesson, Chaim, but what does it have to do with my helping the new neighbors?"

"Avi, don't ever think that you cannot make a difference. Every mitzvah that you do is felt and noticed by those around you. Just like Yaakov Avinu's presence was missed when he left Be'er Sheva, your presence will be missed at the new neighbors' home. We need you and want you to help."

"Chaim, I'm on my way. Sixteen guys helping is a whole lot better than fifteen guys. See you there!"

Simcha's Brain Teaser

Chavi promised Leah today that she will tell Leah a big secret on the day before four days from the day after tomorrow. If today is Shabbos the 12th, on what day and date will Chavi tell Leah her big secret?

For the answer, turn to the back of the book.

Parashas Vayishlach

Lacking Nothing

Whoosh!

"What was that, Avi?"

"I don't know Chaim. It went by so fast, I didn't get a good look at it. Here it comes again!"

Whoosh!

"Wow! Look at that new bicycle! It's really fancy. And really, really fast. Who's riding it?"

"That's Shimon, who lives up the street."

"Shimi, let's see your new bike!"

"Hi guys! Boy, am I out of breath. I'm not used to riding so fast. How do you like my new bike? It's the latest model. I got it for my birthday."

"Wow, Shimi! It looks great. Use it in good health, and be careful. The faster you go, the more you have to watch out. Can I try it?"

"Sure Avi. Don't run over any curbs."

After a short ride, Avi returns with Shimon's new bike.

"Shimi, thanks so much for the ride. That was great. I sure wish I had a bike like that. Enjoy it, Shimi, and happy birthday."

Shimon rides off, and Avi and Chaim continue walking together.

"What do you say about that new bike, Chaim? Don't you wish you had one just like that?"

"Avi, if I'm supposed to have a bike like that, I'm sure I'll get one. If I don't, then it's not the right bike for me."

"I'm not exactly sure what you mean, Chaim. That bike would be great for anybody."

"Maybe not, Avi. Someone who cannot ride well might really hurt himself on such a bike. Let me tell you a story that my teacher told us yesterday. One of our great rabbis, Rav Eliyahu Lopian, tells a story to show how we have everything that we need. A certain man once bragged to his friend about the expensive merchandise that he owned. 'What sort of merchandise is it?' the friend asked. The man led him to a cabinet full of medicines. He explained that the doctor had told him to take these medicines. They were very expensive, and very rare, imported from all over the world. The entire time that the owner was bragging about his medicine collection, his friend was thinking, 'How fortunate am I that I don't need all of this.' Although people are naturally jealous of other's possessions, no one would be jealous of having all of those medicines.

"Rav Lopian quotes the verse that we say in *Birkas HaMazon*, 'Those who seek Hashem are lacking no good.' It does not say that those who seek Hashem have all of the good things in the world. No one can possibly own all of the good things in the world. Rather, they are lacking no good, they have everything they need."

"Chaim, that reminds me of the meeting between Yaakov Avinu and his brother Eisav. We read about it in this week's *parashah*. When they greeted each other after many years of separation, each described his accomplishments."

"What did they say to each other, Avi?"

"Eisav said, 'I have a lot.' Rashi explains, 'Much more than I need.' Although his needs were filled, he kept acquiring more and more. His desires were never satisfied. Yaakov, on the other hand, said, 'I have everything.' How is it possible to own everything? It is not possible. He had everything that he needed. What he did not need, he did not have. He knew that if Hashem wanted him to have something, He would have given it to him.

"So we both realize, Chaim, that if we are supposed to have a fancy bike like Shimon's, then we will get one. And if we don't, then it's just not the right bike for us."

"Avi, with an outlook like that, you will be pedaling very happily through life."

Simcha's Brain Teaser

Nachum once bought a bicycle from a man who was as dishonest as Lavan, the father-in-law of Yaakov Avinu. When Nachum asked how much the bike costs, the man told him, "Not very much. Just pay me one penny today, two pennies tomorrow, four cents the next day, and eight cents the day after, for twenty days." How much did Nachum end up paying for the bicycle after twenty days?

For the answer, turn to the back of the book.

Parashas Vayeishev

Good News Campaign

Extra! Extra! Read all about it! Big, big news break! Read all about it!"

"What's the news break, sir? A hurricane in South America?"

"No."

"An earthquake in California?"

"No."

"Fighting in Angola?"

"Guess again."

"Political scandal?"

"You have one more try, young man."

"I give up, sir."

"Yesterday, a young lady performed a wonderful and amazing act of kindness. She organized a group of girls to pay hospital visits and bring flowers to over one hundred sick patients in one day!"

"That's news?"

"It surely is, young man. Hospital patients know how lonely and depressing a stay in the hospital can be. A visit brightens up the person's whole day. Not only that, it even helps the patient's healing process. And bringing flowers is just the icing on the cake. Beautiful flowers spruce up the hospital room. This young woman performed an extraordinary feat, brightening the lives of one hundred hospital patients."

"But, sir, I thought things like that did not make news."

"What is your name, young man?"

"Chaim."

"Chaim, let me tell you a story from the *parashas hashavua, Vayeishev.* Yosef HaTzaddik, our righteous ancestor, was one of twelve sons of Yaakov. His brothers plotted to kill him. Reuven, the oldest brother, convinced the others to lower Yosef into a pit instead of killing him. His plan was to return to the pit, take Yosef out, and return him to their father, Yaakov. His plan failed because the other brothers drew Yosef out of the pit and sold him to band of passing travelers."

"Reuven had a good idea, but it flopped."

"That's right, Chaim. The great Torah scholar Rabbi Baruch Halevi Epstein, who is known to us as the Torah Temimah, has a wonderful insight. He asks the following question: 'Why did the Torah mention Reuven's plan if it failed?' He answers that it is fitting to praise someone who does a good deed. One should always praise good deeds and the people who perform them. Even in Reuven's case, where the plan failed, the Torah praises him for his efforts."

"Wow, if the Torah honors good deeds, I suppose we should, too."

"Right you are, Chaim. That's why I started this good news campaign. Why should the news always be bad events? Let us do as the Torah does and publicize good things. Will you help me spread the good news?"

"I sure will, sir."

"Hey Avi, guess what? Did you hear the news?"

"Oh no, Chaim, what happened now?"

"Avi, have I got a surprise for you..."

Simcha's Brain Teaser

A snail once fell to the bottom of a pit ten feet deep. The snail was able to climb up three feet every day. Unfortunately, he slid back down two feet every night. How many days did it take him to get out of the pit?

For the answer, turn to the back of the book.

Parashas Mikeitz

Don't Let the Conductor
Fool You

"All aboard! All aboard! Train number 593 leaving for Boston on track number seventeen in ten minutes, at 3:15! All aboard!"

"Avi, look at this! Did you ever see so many trains in your life?"

"Is this your first time at the train station, Chaim?"

"It sure is."

"It is quite overwhelming the first time. The station is so big and busy."

"All aboard! All aboard! Train number 593 leaving for Boston on track number seventeen in five minutes, at 3:15! All aboard!"

"Avi, look at all of those people rushing towards that train bound for Boston. I hope they all make it. They have less than five minutes until it leaves."

"Last call! Train number 593 leaving for Boston on track number seventeen right now! All aboard!"

With that, the big train, filled with people and luggage, pulls slowly away from the platform. Chaim and Avi are fascinated by the surroundings. They watch several other trains load and depart the station. Each train leaves with the same scenario: the conductor shouting "All aboard" three times, and the train pulling away after the last call.

"Avi, that man must be very important. When he gives the word, the trains leave the station. Come, I want to ask him a few questions.

"Excuse me sir. It is a great privilege and honor to meet you. I am sorry to disturb you. May I interrupt your most important work to ask you a few questions?"

"Go right ahead, young man."

"Can you please tell me what is the maximum speed of the train, and how many cars the locomotive can pull, and how long it can go without refueling, and how many passengers each car can carry, and..."

"I am sorry to interrupt you, young man. These are all very good questions and I am sure you have many more, but I cannot answer them."

"Really? Why not?"

"I really do not know anything about the workings of the trains."

"Excuse me for asking, sir, but you must know. After all, you are the most important person in the train station. It is clear that you are supervising the whole operation here. You tell each train when to leave."

"Young man, I am very flattered by what you are saying, but I am afraid you have it all wrong. I am just the lowly conductor. The station manager runs this train station. He sits up in the office. He never comes down here to the platform. I carry out his orders. He gives me the schedule and I just announce when each train leaves. They leave based on the station manager's directions, not mine."

"But I was so sure that you were in charge."

"That is because you only see what is happening down here. You have never been up to the office."

"Well, thank you very much, sir. Again, I'm sorry to have disturbed you."

"That's quite all right, young man."

Chaim and Avi begin walking home from the train station.

"Can you imagine that, Avi? I thought the conductor was the station manager."

"Believe it our not, Chaim, Rav Yisrael Meir Kagan, the great sage who is known to us as the Chafetz Chaim, says that the train station is a parable for life."

"Really, Avi? In what way?"

"The world that we live in is like the train platform. The different people who appear and cause things to happen are like the conductor. Hashem is symbolized by the station manager. He is really supervising the whole world. He is giving the orders that make things happen. The various 'conductors' in the world carry out His directives. You know, Chaim, our ancestor Yosef HaTzaddik was not fooled as you were. He realized that the conductor was just a conductor."

"How did he realize that?"

"He was tested with a very difficult test, which required

a tremendous amount of self-control on his part."

"Did he pass the test?"

"He certainly did."

"What reward did he receive?"

"He was thrown into prison for twelve years."

"That's terrible!"

"That is what we think, Chaim. However, Yosef HaTzaddik was neither angry with the situation, nor with Hashem. He knew that Hashem had His reasons for this, and he continued to strive to be close to Hashem the entire twelve years that he was in prison."

"Now I see why he is called Yosef HaTzaddik. He was truly a righteous person. Who would have ever thought that we could learn such an important thing from a visit to the train station?"

"That is the point, Chaim. When we pay attention to the Station Manager, we can learn something from every event in our lives."

"All aboard, Avi. We don't want to be late for our Torah studies. The class is about to begin."

Simcha's Brain Teaser

A traveler comes to a fork in the road and does not know how to get to his destination. Two men are standing there. One of them always tells the truth, and the other one always lies. He may ask the men one question to find his way. What question does the man ask these men?

For the answer, turn to the back of the book.

It's Embarrassing to Embarrass

Avi, how are you? It's so good to see you. What's the matter, you look a little upset."

"I'll be okay, Chaim. It's really nothing, I suppose."

"Do you want to talk about it?"

"Well, Chaim, a very embarrassing thing just happened to me."

"*Oy vey.*"

"Yesterday, I told a personal secret to a very good friend. I told him not to tell anyone, because it was very personal. Today, three or four people came to me and asked me about the secret. I was so embarrassed that they knew about it. I feel terrible."

"Avi, now I understand what our Sages wrote in the Talmud. Embarrassing someone is like spilling their blood. I see how awful you feel from the embarrassment. You know, Avi, we can learn a lesson from everything that happens to us in life. We can learn never to embarrass anyone."

"Chaim, do you know that our ancestor Yosef HaTzaddik put his own life in danger to avoid embarrassing his brothers?"

"Really? What happened?"

"Here is the scenario: Yosef's brothers stood in front of the leader of Mitzrayim, his servants, and his guards. Little did they know that this powerful ruler was none other than their own brother Yosef, whom they had sold as a slave to a band of travelers many years earlier. He had made his way to Mitzrayim and had risen to the position of second-in-command to the king. In his capacity as ruler, Yosef had treated his brothers harshly, giving them good reason to resent him. Now, he realized that the time had come to reveal his identity to his brothers. What should he do? To divulge his secret in the presence of the Mitzrim would cause his brothers great shame and embarrassment. It would become public knowledge that they once sold their own brother as a slave, a shameful act. To send all of the Mitzri guards out of the room would be very dangerous. Yosef would be alone with the people whom he had treated so harshly. If the brothers chose to kill him, no one could stop them."

"Tell me, Avi, how did Yosef deal with this dilemma?"

"Chaim, our Sages tell us, 'It is better for a person to throw himself into a fiery furnace than to shame someone in public.' Yosef HaTzaddik risked danger to his own life rather than humiliate his brothers."

"Avi, the righteous deeds of our forefathers are a role model for our behavior. I will try never to embarrass, shame, or humiliate anyone."

"Chaim, you are great. Hashem should reward you that you should never suffer embarrassment yourself."

Simcha's Brain Teaser

An Indian guru tells his two sons to race their camels to a distant city to see who will inherit his fortune. The one whose camel is slower will win. The brothers, after wandering aimlessly for days, ask a wise man for advice. After hearing the advice they jump on the camels and race as fast as they can to the city. What does the wise man say?

For the answer, turn to the back of the book.

Parashas Vayechi

Smile!

"Shhh...Daddy's coming. Let's all give him the most wonderful welcome of his life."

Knock knock. "I'm home."

"Shalom, Daddy! How are you? It's great to see you! How was your day? Come in, relax. Have something to drink. What can we bring you? We're so happy you're home!"

"What a marvelous reception! Ahuva, you're smiling so sweetly. It really warms my heart. Moishie, I see all of your beautiful white teeth. What a handsome smile you have. Leah, do you know how much prettier you look when you smile? Avi, your smile comes straight from the heart. Mommy, you are smiling as warmly as on the day I married you."

"Daddy, we wanted to give you the best welcome of your life."

"To what do I owe the honor of this extraordinary welcome?"

"We learned all about the importance of smiling in our

parashas hashavua class, Daddy."

"Really! Please tell me about it."

"Yaakov Avinu, at the end of his life, gave blessings to his sons. Each of Yaakov's twelve sons received his own individual blessing. Part of the blessing given to Yehudah was, 'His eyes are red with wine, and his teeth are white with milk' (Bereishis 49:12). The Talmud teaches us a very important lesson based on this verse: It is better to whiten your teeth to your friend (smile to him) than to pour milk for him. We all know how important it is to serve our guests food and drink when they arrive. We learn that from Avraham Avinu. He literally ran to serve his guests. Now we learn that smiling is even more important."

"That is truly amazing, kids."

"May I add to what you learned?"

"Sure, Mommy."

"There are two passages in *Pirkei Avos* which tell us of the importance of smiling. The first is in the very first chapter: 'Shammai says...receive everyone with a beautiful facial expression.' Also in the third chapter: 'Rebbe Yishmael says...receive everyone with happiness.' Children, it is so important to greet people with a smile. Let us count how many mitzvos we receive when we smile."

"I know one!"

"Yes, Avi."

"We make people happy, which is a true act of kindness."

"Correct!"

"I have another one."

"Yes, Leah."

"We can help make peace between people."

"Very good!"

"What do you want to say, Ahuva?"

"We make Hashem happy."

"You're so right. When we are happy, He is happy."

"Let's all keep smiling, and smiling, and smiling away!"

Simcha's Brain Teaser

You buy nine oranges at the market. All of the oranges look exactly alike, and eight of them weigh the same, but one of them is heavier than the others. You want to weigh them to know which is the heavy one, but the fruit seller, with his old-fashioned scales (with 2 weighing pans), will allow you to weigh only twice. How do you do it?

For the answer, turn to the back of the book.

Shemos

Parashas Shemos

Prized Possession

"Avi, come! Do you want to go with me to the bank this morning?"

"Sure, Mommy."

"Get ready quickly. I have to leave in five minutes."

"Okay, Mommy. I'm ready to go now. What are we going to do at the bank?"

"I need to get something from the safe-deposit box, Avi."

"What is a safe-deposit box, Mommy?"

"It is a locked box in the vault of the bank, where people keep very valuable possessions."

"I'm excited, Mommy. I've never seen a vault or a safe-deposit box before."

At the bank...

"I'm afraid you will have to wait a few minutes, ma'am, until one of the rooms becomes free."

"What room is the man speaking about, Mommy?"

"Each person takes his safe-deposit box into a small

room, where he can examine its contents in private. All of the rooms are occupied, so we'll have to wait."

"Excuse me, sir."

"Yes, young man."

"Can you tell me why it is so busy here today? Why are none of the rooms free?"

"Young man, there are certain people who come here every day."

"Really? Every day? What do they do?"

"They take out their safe-deposit box and count their money. They have their life's savings in the box, and they come here and count the money every day."

"Don't they get bored?"

"Apparently not. They worked so hard for their money that they became very attached to it. It is their greatest pleasure to count, count, and recount their most prized possession. Look at that. As we are talking, one of the rooms has become free. You may go in, ma'am."

On the way home from the bank...

"Can you imagine that, Mommy? People count and recount their money every day."

"You know, Avi, this can give you an insight into this week's *parashah*. The Book of Shemos begins with a listing of the names of the Jews who went down to Mitzrayim. Rashi makes an interesting observation. Hashem had listed the names of those very same Jews who went down to Mitzrayim only a short time ago at the end of the Book of Bereishis. Why did He list them again here? The answer is that the Jewish people are very dear to Him. We are like His prized possession. Therefore, He enjoys counting us — similar to the way that the man in the bank enjoys counting his valuables."

"Wow, Mommy! Who would ever think that you could learn something from a trip to the bank?"

"Avi, inspiration is everywhere if you look for it. You should know that Hashem still loves us as much as He did then. Each and every one of us, including you, are one of His very special prized possessions."

"Mommy, you always know the right thing to say!"

Simcha's Brain Teaser

If TEN = 10-5-14,
and MEN = 13-5-14,
what do WOMEN equal by the same logic?

For the answer, turn to the back of the book.

Gratitude

Knock, knock. "Mommy, I'm home."
"Chaim, how are you? How was school today?"

"Great, Mommy. Guess what?"

"What, Chaim."

"I got an invitation from Avi to sleep over at his house this Shabbos. Can I go?"

"We'll check it out with Daddy when he comes home. Until then Chaim, start on your homework."

"Okay, Mommy."

Later that evening...

"Hi, everyone. I'm home."

"Hi Daddy. We're all so happy to see you!"

"Daddy, guess what? Avi invited me to sleep over at his house this Shabbos. Can I go?"

"Let me discuss this with Mommy, Chaim."

A short time later...

"Chaim, you can go to Avi's for Shabbos."

"Great!"

"Just remember one thing."

"What's that, Daddy?"

"His family are opening their home to you. You must make sure to thank them properly for their hospitality. I have a great story about hospitality. Do you want to hear it?"

"Sure, Daddy."

"It is about the great scholar Rav Levi Yitzchak of Berdichev. He was traveling in Eastern Europe and arrived at a small town one evening. He went from house to house looking for a place to stay. No one recognized the Rav, and he was turned away from each home. He tried every home in the town and received the same depressing answer.

"Finally, there remained only one house, the run-down home of a poor man. Rav Levi Yitzchak knocked on the door and asked for a place to sleep that night. The owner replied that he was only a poor man with a simple home. If the traveler would not mind staying in such poor surroundings, he would be honored to host him for the night. Rav Levi Yitzchak gladly accepted the invitation, stayed the night, and thanked him profusely when he left the next day.

"Some years later, when Rav Levi Yitzchak became known far and wide as a great scholar and a tzaddik, he returned to the town for a visit. The residents all competed for the honor of hosting the Torah leader in their homes. Rav Levi Yitzchak shook his head. 'I will stay with the poor man at the edge of town, if he will admit me,' he announced. 'It was he who took me in the last time, and it is to him that I must express my everlasting gratitude. Once someone performs a favor for you, you must never forget it.' "

"Wow, Daddy, that's a great story!"

"Really, Chaim, we have another example of gratitude from this week's *parashah*."

"I'll bet I can guess who it involves."

"Okay, Chaim, go ahead."

"Moshe Rabbeinu."

"Very good, Chaim! Do you know how he showed his gratitude?"

"I sure do, Daddy. It was during the ten plagues. The first two plagues of blood and frogs involved the Nile River. That very same river saved Moshe when he was a baby. The Mitzrim wanted to kill him and all of the baby boys. To save him, his mother put him in a basket and set him afloat on the river. He was only three months old at the time. He floated down the river a bit, then Batya, the daughter of Pharaoh, saw him and took him home with her. The Nile River saved his life."

"Where does his gratitude come into the story, Chaim?"

"Moshe Rabbeinu did not begin the first two plagues. His brother Aharon stretched his staff over the river and it turned to blood. He also used his staff to bring frogs out of the river. Moshe was not commanded to do this because he owed the Nile River a debt of gratitude for saving his life."

"Very good, Chaim!"

"But Daddy, I have one question."

"Sure, Chaim."

"The river is not alive. It cannot appreciate Moshe's gratitude."

"Excellent, Chaim. This shows us how important gratitude is. If we must have gratitude to an inanimate object which cannot see or feel, how much more so to a living human being. Gratitude and appreciation are one of the foundations of relationships. So you see, Chaim, it is very important to express appreciation to Avi and his family."

"Daddy, I can only say 'thank you' to you for teaching me the importance of saying 'thank you.' "

Simcha's Brain Teaser

One train leaves from NYC heading towards LA at 100 mph. Three hours later, a train leaves from LA heading towards NYC at 200 mph. Assume there's exactly 2000 miles between LA and NYC. When they meet, which train is closer to NYC.

For the answer, turn to the back of the book.

Parashas Bo

Follow Me

Ssssssst...

"What was that, Avi?"

"It sounded like a snake, Chaim. There! Look at it! It's going under that rock! Wow, can it move fast!"

"I'm scared. I never should have gone on this tour of the desert."

"Let's ask the tour guide if there is anything to be afraid of, Chaim."

"Excuse me, Mr. Tour Guide, we just saw a snake. Is it dangerous?"

"It depends on what type of snake, boys. We had better all get back into the tour bus as a safety precaution. Everyone, back into the bus! A snake has been sighted!"

"Mr. Tour Guide, the desert seems like a really dangerous place."

"That's correct, young man. There are snakes and scorpions whose sting can kill a person. There is no water to drink. A person can dehydrate in a matter of a few hours. The sun is very strong. Without proper protection, a person can get sunstroke. There is no shade. There is also no food. The desert is no place for people, unless they have plenty of supplies and protection."

"Did you know, Mr. Tour Guide, that our ancestors went out of the land of Mitzrayim into the desert?"

"Yes, young man. That is a famous Bible story."

"Mr. Tour Guide, this is my first time in a desert. Until now, I never really appreciated what happened to our ancestors over three thousand years ago."

"What do you mean, young man?"

"Well, Mitzrayim was a very fertile and settled land. The last of Hashem's ten plagues was 'death of the firstborn.' That resulted in Pharaoh freeing the Jewish slaves. Over two million men, women, and children were now free to settle in the land of Mitzrayim. But Hashem had a different plan. 'Follow Me into the wilderness, into an unsown land' (Yirmeyahu 2:2). Where? The wilderness? Two million men, women, and children (including old and sick people)? What will they eat? What will they drink? Do you know how much food two million people eat? Where will they find shelter?

What about snakes and scorpions? Go into the wilderness? It sounds suicidal. Yet our ancestors did it out of love for Hashem and appreciation for all that He had done for them. Do you know what? He performed miracle after miracle, sustaining and protecting those two million people in this un-livable desert."

"Young man, you have painted quite a vivid picture of the Exodus. I never really thought deeply into it."

"Well, sir, neither did I until I experienced this desert wilderness. This has added a new dimension to my appreciation of the many miracles and acts of kindness that Hashem has done for the Jewish people."

Simcha's Brain Teaser

If two hours ago it was as long after one o'clock in the afternoon as it was before one o'clock in the morning. What time would it be now?

For the answer, turn to the back of the book.

Parashas Beshalach

You Were There

"Father, I'm cold. The wind is blowing very hard."

"Come close to me, my son, and I will try to keep you warm."

"Father, I'm scared. What are we going to do? We are trapped. The sea is in front of us, the Mitzrim are behind us, and there are wild animals from the desert on both sides of us. Where can we go?"

"My son, some say that we should return to Mitzrayim and go back to slavery. They say that it is better to live as a slave than to die here in the desert. Others say that we should fight the Mitzrim right here and now. Still others say that we should make loud noises to frighten them off. The last group says that we should throw ourselves into the sea. It is better to trust in the compassion of the Merciful One than to fall to the hands of our enemies."

"Father, what are we going to do?"

"My son, let us listen to our leader, Moshe Rabbeinu. He is speaking now."

"*Do not fear. Stand fast and see the salvation of Hashem*

that He will perform for you today. As you see Mitzrayim to-day, you will never see them again!"

"Father, look! Someone is entering the sea! Who is he?"

"That is Nachshon ben Aminadav, the prince of the tribe of Yehudah."

"Father, all of his tribe are following him into the sea! They are signaling for all of us to follow them."

"Come, my son. Do not be afraid. Trust in Hashem."

"Father, the water is cold. It is almost up to my nose. Soon I will not be able to breathe."

"Look, my son! The water is splitting and running away from us. It is piling up, forming huge walls on either side of us. And look, the strong wind is drying out the floor of the sea beneath our feet! There are pillars of fire and clouds behind us, protecting us from the Mitzrim."

"Father, Hashem is saving us."

"Come, my son, let us move forward. In front of us are twelve tunnels. Let us follow the members of our tribe into the tunnel made especially for us."

"Father, look! It's beautiful in here. The floor is smooth and polished like marble. The walls sparkle like sapphires and diamonds. Look, I can see my friends in the next tunnel through the wall. Father, I'm hungry. It's been so long since we've eaten."

"Look, my son. There are beautiful fruit trees here in the tunnel. Let me pick a fruit for you to eat."

"Yum, that apple sure was delicious. I'm sorry, Father, but now I am so thirsty."

"Here, my son, just touch the wall of the tunnel, and

sparkling clear water comes flowing out."

"Oh, no, I don't want to make a leak in the tunnel, Father."

"Don't worry, my son. When you are finished, the hole will seal up again."

"Father, there is such a beautiful fragrance in here, not like the smell of the sea at all."

"My son, Hashem is giving us a real treat. He is making it beautiful for us in here. The travel is so easy. The floor is smooth and level. Even the old people and little children are keeping pace. Hashem, with His infinite kindness, has even provided food for our cattle here. My son, enjoy our trip through the sea. But pay attention and remember. This is an experience not to be forgotten. I am sure that you will want to share it with your children and grandchildren."

"Thank you so much, Father."

Now, back to our seder table...

"And so, children, that was how it happened — *kriyas Yam Suf*, the splitting of the Red Sea."

"Daddy, you really make it come alive. You put in so many details. It is as if you were really there."

"Children, the Haggadah states: 'In each and every generation, a person is obligated to see himself as if he went out of Mitzrayim. As it states in the Torah, "And you shall tell your son on that day saying, 'For this, Hashem did for me when I went out of Mitzrayim.' " Not only did Hashem redeem our forefathers, but He redeemed us with them.'

"When I tell you the story, we must feel that we were there. That is how we fulfill the mitzvah of *sipur yetzias Mitzrayim*."

"Thank you, Daddy. Your master storytelling and Mommy's delicious cooking have made this our best Pesach seder ever!"

Simcha's Brain Teaser

A man has to get a fox, a chicken, and a sack of corn across a river. He has a rowboat, and it can only carry him and one other thing. If the fox and the chicken are left together, the fox will eat the chicken. If the chicken and the corn are left together, the chicken will eat the corn. How does the man do it?

For the answer, turn to the back of the book.

Follow the Directions Carefully

Wow, Avi, what's that?"

"It's a gift that I just received from my parents, Chaim."

"It looks really neat. What is it?"

"An electronic, battery powered, cordless, 1000x magnification microscope. With it, we can see all kinds of microscopic objects invisible to the naked eye. It's so new, it's still in the box."

"Let's open it up, Avi."

"Sure, Chaim. But what's this on the outside of the box?"

Caution. This is a very delicate instrument. Do not attempt to open or operate this microscope before reading the instructions carefully.

"We had better read the instructions first, Chaim, before we open the box. I sure wouldn't want to damage this beautiful new microscope in any way. I've wanted one for a long time. My parents just bought it for me. Until now, they said that I wasn't old enough to have such a delicate instrument."

"Of course, Avi, but what's the big deal? We open it up, put the batteries in, and turn it on. Then we can see all kinds of neat things, like blades of grass, insects, microbes..."

"But Chaim, what if we press the wrong button, or drip water in the wrong place? We could ruin the whole thing."

"I guess you're right, Avi. Any time you are dealing with something complicated, you have to follow the instruction manual to operate it properly. You know, Avi, the Jewish people received the instruction manual in this week's *parashah*."

"What do you mean, Chaim?"

"This week is *parashas Yisro*. It includes the giving of the Torah on Har Sinai."

"Great, Chaim. But what does that have to do with an instruction manual?"

"Avi, you may think that a microscope is complicated and delicate. But it is just a crude instrument compared to a human being. After all, how many parts does that microscope have? Twenty? Fifty? A hundred? Even if it has a thousand parts, the human body has billions and billions of cells, which make up complicated tissues, nerves, muscles, and organs. Scientists and doctors are just beginning to fathom the complexity of the human body. There are a million and one things that can go wrong with the human being. We need to know how to take proper care of ourselves physically. How to eat, sleep, exercise, and dress properly, among other things. We surely wouldn't want to damage the wonderful body that we have by not following the instruction manual.

"However, that is just the physical side. There is also the soul, which is a very delicate thing indeed. It has the potential for greatness. We have to know how to nurture it so that we can grow and use all of our skills to their fullest. We all have talents in different areas, and to waste them is really damaging our wonderful gifts. We've got to follow the instruction manual."

"Chaim, that's very scary. How can we possibly know what to do? Who can understand the human being well enough to give the proper instructions?"

"Well, let's see, Avi. Who wrote the instruction manual for this microscope?"

"That's easy, Chaim. The people who made it. They know how it works."

"Who made the human being, Avi? Who knows how it works?"

"Hashem did."

"Guess what? He also wrote the instruction manual. It's called the Torah. The Torah is a book written by Hashem about man, giving us the instructions we need to live our lives properly. If we follow the instructions written in the Torah, we won't damage the delicate instrument that Hashem has given us."

"Chaim, you've magnified my view of life 1000 times without even opening the box of this microscope!"

Simcha's Brain Teaser

How many mitzvos are in the Ten Commandments?

For the answer, turn to the back of the book.

Parashas Mishpatim

Turn It Around

Hi, Avi! How are you?"

"Fine, Chaim, *baruch Hashem*. How are you?"

"The same, *baruch Hashem*. Do you want to join us for a game of basketball?"

"Sure, Chaim."

"Hi, Josh! How are you?"

"Great, guys! What's doing?"

"We're on our way to play basketball. Do you want to come?"

"I can't right now. Thanks for asking. Have a good time."

On the way home from the basketball game...

"Look, Avi, isn't that Josh?"

"Sure is. And I think that's Aharon with him. They're both walking behind Rabbi Finkel. What are they doing?"

"It looks like they are both carrying a heavy load of books for Rabbi Finkel. Come, let's go help them out."

"You go help Josh, and I'll help Aharon. I'd rather not help Josh."

"Why not, Avi?"

"Do you want to know the truth, Chaim?"

"Of course."

"I was really happy when Josh didn't want to play with us today. The last few times we played basketball together, he was always banging into me and stepping on my feet. It really bothers me. Can't he be more careful? He didn't even apologize. I'd rather not help him carry the books. I would rather help Aharon, my friend."

"Avi, do you know that the Torah says to do exactly the opposite?"

"It can't be."

"It's right in this week's *parashah, Mishpatim.*"

"Really? What does it say, Chaim?"

"When you see two people who need help, and one is your friend and the other is not your friend, you should go help the one you're not friendly with first."

"But I want to help my friend. I like him. I don't like the other guy."

"That's exactly the point, Avi. There is a mitzvah in the Torah to love all of our brethren. That includes even those who treat us not so nicely. The Torah is teaching us how to turn around your bad feelings toward that person. If you help him, if you give to him, you will come to like him."

"How does that work?"

"The more you give to him, the more you feel for him. You identify more closely with him because you have put effort into him."

"Kind of like a project."

"In a way, but much more. The biggest proof is our parents. They love us so much because they have put so much effort into raising us."

"I see the point, Chaim. I guess the hardest part is to get started."

"It's like jumping into the pool, Avi. Just hold your breath and take the plunge."

"Okay, here goes... Hey, Josh, can I help you with those heavy books?"

"Why, that is so nice of you, Avi. I guess I took too many books. You know, Avi, I have been meaning to tell you what a good basketball player you are. You are so graceful, you never bump into anybody or step on their feet. I wish I could play like you."

"Maybe I can help you play better, Josh. Together we can turn it around."

Simcha's Brain Teaser

How much dirt is in a hole that is 3 feet deep and 6 inches in diameter?

For the answer, turn to the back of the book.

Get More Than You Give

Good afternoon, boys! How are you?"

"Fine, *baruch Hashem*, Mr. Grant, how are you?"

"Good. You boys look like you're full of pep and energy. Do you think that you can do a little work for me?"

"What do you have in mind, Mr. Grant?"

"Come with me and I'll show you. Of course I will pay you for your work."

"Thank you very much, Mr. Grant."

"Do you see that pit there in the middle of my garden?"

"Yes."

"I need to fill it up with dirt. This morning, a truck came and delivered a whole pile of dirt to fill up the pit. The only problem is they dumped it on the other side of the garden. Here are a couple of buckets and shovels. I would like you to shovel dirt into the bucket, carry the bucket over to the pit, and dump the dirt into the pit. Hopefully, before long the pit will be filled. Now, boys, I'm going to pay you a dime for every bucket of dirt that you move. I just don't have a lot of dimes. I do have a whole bag of pennies. After you dump each bucket, come over to me and I'll give you a penny. At the end of the job, we'll count the pennies, multiply by ten, and I'll give you all of your money. Okay?"

"Fair enough, Mr. Grant. When can we start.?"

"Right now."

"Great!"

And so, the boys began working...

"Chaim, this is great exercise."

"Right, Avi. And we're helping Mr. Grant."

"We're also getting paid. How many pennies do you have so far, Chaim?"

"Ten."

"That's a whole dollar."

After about one hour of hard work...

"Avi, I sure am getting thirsty."

"Me too, Chaim."

"Maybe we can take a break and get something to drink. There's a store right up the street. I could sure go for an ice-cold lemonade."

"Sounds like a great idea, Chaim. The only problem is that I don't have any money."

"Neither do I, Avi. Wait a minute, I have a whole pocketful of pennies."

"Me too, Chaim. How many do you have? Let's count them."

"I have twenty-five pennies, Avi."

"I also have twenty-five, Chaim. Together, that's

enough for a lemonade. Let's go."

"Wait a minute, Avi. I just thought of something."

"What's that?"

"For each of these pennies we will receive ten cents after the job is over. If we wait till we finish, we'll have five dollars, not fifty cents."

"I'm thirsty, Chaim."

"I am too, Avi. But if we just persevere, we will be able to buy ten lemonades!"

"I'm thirsty, Chaim."

"Let me tell you something about this week's *parashah*, which is very relevant to our little job here."

"What do you mean?"

"Hashem commands the Jewish people, saying, 'Take *terumah* for Me.' "

"What's *terumah*?"

"That is the name given to the gifts that the Jewish people gave to Hashem. He asked them to donate the raw materials necessary to build the *mishkan* in the desert. They followed His wishes and gave very generously."

"But Chaim, I thought you said the commandment was to 'take *terumah*,' not to 'give *terumah*.' "

"Exactly, Avi. Hashem should have used the word 'give.' Instead He used the word 'take' to teach us something. Whenever we give to Hashem, we are really taking."

"In what way, Chaim?"

"When we give charity to a poor person, we are receiving more than we give. When we give of our time to visit the sick, we are receiving more than we give. When we invest our mental energies into learning and teaching Torah, we are receiving more than we give."

"What are we receiving, Chaim?"

"The reward that we receive for these mitzvos is far greater than the time, effort, or money that we give. It's just like Mr. Grant. We give him a penny and we receive a dime in return. Would anyone ever think of spending that penny at the store? Of course not! We receive much more for that penny from Mr. Grant than the store will ever give us. So, too, the reward that Hashem gives us for giving charity is far greater than anything that we could have bought with that money."

"Look at that, Chaim. As we were talking, we finished the job. Let's go hand in the pennies and get our reward."

"I'm right with you, Avi. I can taste that ice-cold lemonade already."

Simcha's Brain Teaser

You throw away the outside and cook the inside. Then you eat the outside and throw away the inside. What did you eat?

For the answer, turn to the back of the book.

Take It into Your Heart

Aand now the 9:00 news, brought to you by station WBBB — the final decision has been handed down by the High Court. Governor I. B. Ganiff has been convicted and sentenced on ten counts of bribery, extortion, theft, and grand larceny. And now for the weather..."

"Did you hear that, Avi?"

"Sure, Chaim. Who is this Governor Ganiff? The name sounds so familiar. Ganiff, Ganiff, Ganiff..."

"Avi, is that Governor I. Binna Ganiff?"

"The name sounds right, Chaim. Where do I know that name?"

"He ran for office a few years ago. During his election campaign, he promised to fight corruption in government. He made speech after speech about the importance of honesty and integrity in government. He coined the slogan, 'I. B. G. stands for honesty.'

"And now he has been convicted on ten counts of bribery, extortion, theft, and grand larceny. Imagine that. When he was running for office, he seemed so knowledgeable on the subject of corruption, and so sincere in his commitment to fight it. Now we see that it was all just talk. He has proven to be a real disappointment."

"Chaim, a person's knowledge does not always govern his actions. Governor Ganiff is very well educated in the subject of fighting corruption. However, that did not stop him from stealing himself. He may be very smart and knowledgeable, but he is not a wise man."

"What do you mean, Avi?"

"The Torah uses the expression 'chacham-leiv' in this week's *parashah, Tetzaveh.* The words seem to be a contra-

diction. 'Chacham' usually refers to a person's knowledge. That is stored in the head, in the brain. 'Leiv' is the word for heart. The heart is the seat of the emotions and desires. 'Chacham-leiv' means a wise heart. But how can the heart be wise? The head is wise, not the heart."

"Good question, Avi. What's the answer?"

"A *chacham-leiv* is someone who takes to heart the wisdom that he has learned. He lets wisdom govern his heart. If he knows something is right, he will do it. If he knows something is wrong, he will stay far away from it. A *chacham-leiv* is a living example of what he has learned. A *chacham-leiv* who is an expert on corruption would never steal, bribe, or extort money. His integrity would be as solid as his knowledge."

"Wow, Avi! This puts a whole new light on our Torah learning. I am going to try to put into practice everything that I learn."

"I see that you're starting right now, Chaim. You learned how important it is to put into practice what you learn, and you are already putting that piece of knowledge into practice. You're a real *chacham-leiv*."

Simcha's Brain Teaser

A genuis came to a narrow railroad bridge and began to run across it. He had crossed 3/8 of the distance when a whistle behind him warned of an approaching train. Being a genius, he instantly evaluated his alternatives. If he were to run back to the beginning of the bridge at his speed of 10 mph, he would leave the bridge at precisely the moment the train entered it. If he kept on running to the end of the bridge, the train would reach him just as he left the bridge. At what speed was the train moving?

For the answer, turn to the back of the book.

Uncountable

Do you have a minyan yet, Chaim? Let's count. One, two, three."

"We shouldn't do that, Avi."

"Do what?"

"Count Jews like that. It is customary to count Jews with the words of a verse, or using objects."

"I'm confused, Chaim. Can you explain what you're talking about?"

"Look in this week's parashah, Avi. Moshe Rabbeinu counted the Jews using half-shekel coins. Each person gave a half-shekel. Moshe counted all of the money, multiplied the shekels by two, and came up with the number of Jews."

"That's a little clearer, Chaim, but I have another question."

"Go ahead."

"Why did Moshe Rabbeinu use half-shekel coins and multiply by two? Wouldn't it have been simpler to use one shekel coins and count them to get the number directly?"

"Avi, that's a famous question asked by many of our great Sages. Each one has his own answer to the question. I will tell you the answer given by the Kesav Sofer, the great Rav of Pressburg: We are all composed of two parts, body and soul. Each part is represented by half a shekel. The two halves together make a whole. The only half that we can count, however, is the body. It is limited and can be counted. The body can only eat or drink so much. Then it must stop. It can only work so long. It can only live so long. It eventually reaches its limits. The soul, however, is unlimited. The soul is the part of us that comes from the heavenly realm. We cannot begin to count it. There is no limit to what the soul can accomplish. It is eternal."

"That's a pretty deep concept, Chaim. Can you give me an example of what you're talking about?"

"Take, for example, the great rav who lived about 250 years ago, Rav Aryeh Leib MeMitz, who is known to us as the Sha'agas Aryeh. He learned through the entire Talmud 1000 times in his life! The Talmud is 2700 pages long. He lived ninety years. If he knew the Talmud by the time he was ten, he had to review the entire Talmud once each month, or about 100 pages each day! That's a pretty mind-boggling feat. Rebbe Akiva Eiger, who lived a little later, also learned 100 pages of Talmud each day."

"Wow!"

"But perhaps the most famous example of phenomenal accomplishment is Rebbe Akiva, the leader of the Jewish people who lived almost 2000 years ago during the time of the Romans. He did not begin learning Torah until he was forty. When he began, he could not even read *alef-beis*. He studied diligently for twenty-four solid years and became the greatest *talmid chacham* of his generation, and indeed one of the greatest of all time. Avi, these people accomplished things far beyond the realm of natural attainment. They showed us the unlimited potential of the soul. The soul cannot be counted. It is unlimited."

"Chaim, those are very encouraging words. There are many times when I feel tired or frustrated or too discouraged to continue. Now that I see what a person is capable of doing, I'll try a little harder. Who knows what hidden potential is inside of me, or you, or Yitzy, or Shmuelik."

"Look at that, Avi, as we were talking, a minyan of men has arrived. Let's all pray to Hashem that we soar with our souls to great achievements."

Simcha's Brain Teaser

A census taker approaches a house and asks the woman who asnweres the door, "How many children do you have, and what are their ages?"

The woman says, "I have three children, the product of their ages is 36, the sum of their ages is equal to the address of the house next door."

The census taker walks next door, comes back, and says, "I need more information."

The woman replies, "I have to go, my oldest child is sleeping upstairs."

The census taker says, "Thank you, I have everything I need."

Question: What are the ages of each of the three children?

For the answer, turn to the back of the book.

No Experience Required

A vi, did you see that sign over there?"
"What sign, Chaim?"
"The sign about volunteers. Look."

Wanted:
Volunteers to lead an afternoon
group for first-grade boys.
Must be at least ten years old.
No experience required.

"Are you thinking about applying, Chaim?"
"Yes, I am. It sounds like a great opportunity. I'm really interested."
"Aren't you scared, Chaim?"
"Of what, Avi?"
"Maybe you won't be able to control the kids."
"But the sign says, 'No experience required.' I guess they'll teach me what to do on the spot."
"Did you ever try to lead little kids before?"
"No."

"They can be pretty energetic."

"But the sign says, 'No experience required,' Avi."

"Okay, I hope you're right."

"Avi, I can tell you another time that people with no experience undertook difficult jobs and succeeded."

"When was that, Chaim?"

"During the building of the *mishkan* in the desert. The Ramban explains the scenario as follows: When the Jewish people were slaves in Mitzrayim, their work consisted of brick making and building construction. They had absolutely no experience working with silver and gold, hewing stones, woodworking, or weaving. Yet these were the skills required to build the mishkan and its accessories. How could they succeed? There were even more difficulties. The jobs required more than the skill of a craftsman. They required great wisdom to understand the complicated and subtle workings of the *mishkan* and its accessories in order to properly fashion them. How could a former slave who worked with crude bricks his whole life ever be able to build the *mishkan*?"

"What's the answer, Chaim?"

"Hashem filled the workers with the wisdom they needed to do the job. All they needed was the desire to succeed. The Torah states (Shemos 35:21), 'Every man whose heart inspired him came [to work]; and everyone whose spirit motivated him...' If they were ready to do whatever Hashem wanted, then He would give them the skills they needed."

"I see, Chaim. It is certainly a big mitzvah to help first-grade boys use their afternoon time productively. If you are prepared to do whatever is needed, you will acquire the necessary skills. If that's the case, I think I'll volunteer also. In fact, this is a good thing to keep in mind for all mitzvos. I won't let my lack of knowledge discourage me. What I need to know, I will learn."

"That's great, Avi. See, you've learned something very important already."

Simcha's Brain Teaser

You have two hour glasses: a 4-minute glass and a 7-minute glass. You want to measure 9 minutes. How do you do it?

For the answer, turn to the back of the book.

Parashas Pekudei

Above Suspicion

Hi, Avi, what are you doing?"

"I'm working for Mr. Levy, helping him stuff envelopes."

"It looks like precise work."

"It is, Chaim. Each package contains one letter, one calendar, and one return envelope. The name on the letter must match the address on the outside of the package. Then I must put a stamp on each one."

"Did you say this is a job, Avi?"

"Yes. When I finish, Mr. Levy will pay me for the number of hours that I worked."

"That sounds great, Avi. Mr. Levy is a smart man. He has hired a great worker. He can rely on you to do the work without his being here to supervise you. He also trusts you to give a correct accounting of the number of hours that you worked."

"To tell you the truth, Chaim, he did not even ask for the number of hours. He just wants to know the amount of money that I earned."

"Wow. He really trusts you, Avi. Even so, I think that you should still report the number of hours to him."

"Why, Chaim? He trusts me."

"I'll tell you, Avi. We learned something in this week's *parashah* about trustworthiness. Would you like me to share it with you?"

"Sure, Chaim."

"Was there anyone more trustworthy than Moshe Rabbeinu?"

"I guess not."

"You don't have to guess, Avi. The Torah writes in Bemidbar 12:7 that Moshe Rabbeinu was Hashem's trusted one."

"Well, Chaim, if Hashem trusted him, then he must have been pretty reliable."

"Right. Do you know the beginning of this week's Torah portion, *parashas Pekudei*?"

"Sure, Chaim. We just learned that today. Moshe Rabbeinu gave an accounting of all of the materials that he collected from *b'nei Yisrael* for the building of the *mishkan*."

"Think about that, Avi. Moshe Rabbeinu gave an accounting. Do you think anyone suspected him of stealing anything? Moshe Rabbeinu was so honest that Hashem trusted him. Why did he have to give an accounting?"

"You're right, Chaim. That does sound a little strange."

"The *midrash* answers this question, Avi, by explaining the following. Just as a person has to work at being honest and trusted by Hashem, so too he must prove his trustworthiness to his fellowman. Hashem knows everything, and

Hashem trusted Moshe Rabbeinu. Therefore he was surely honest. Still, he had to give an accounting to his fellow Jews in order to be above suspicion."

"Wow, Chaim. It must be really important to be above suspicion."

"It sure is, Avi."

"Well, I am going to report my hours and work in exact detail to Mr. Levy. Even though he trusts me, I am going to be like Moshe Rabbeinu. I am going to place myself above suspicion."

"Avi, I would never suspect you of doing anything less."

Simcha's Brain Teaser

Aharon wrote all the numbers from 300 to 400 on a piece of paper. How many times did he write the digit 3?

For the answer, turn to the back of the book.

Vayikra

The Most Humble of All

H i guys!"

"Hi Josh!"

"Guess what? I just got back my math test. Did you know that I got 105 percent?"

"Wow, Josh."

"Not only did I get all of the questions right, I also answered the extra-credit questions correctly."

"Great, Josh."

"I'm on my way to basketball practice. I'm the leading scorer on the team."

"Fantastic, Josh."

"After that, I think I'll stop off at my math teacher's house. It's on the way home."

"Did he ask you to come by?"

"No, but considering I'm the top student in the class, I figure that he'll be happy to see me. See you later, guys!"

"Bye, Josh."

"Well, Chaim, Josh certainly has many accomplishments to be proud of."

"Yes, Avi. He is a very talented person."

"Do you know that our rebbe was teaching us about Moshe Rabbeinu's accomplishments this week?"

"Really? Which ones did he speak about?"

"He quoted the commentary of the *Midrash Rabba* on this week's *parashah*, *Vayikra*. Moshe was the 'Father of Wisdom,' the most intelligent and wise person of his time. He was the 'Father of the Prophets,' who reached the closest level possible to Hashem. He led the Jewish people out of Mitzrayim. Hashem utilized him to perform many miracles in Mitzrayim and at the Red Sea. He rose to the highest heights and brought the Torah down from heaven to earth. He worked on the building of the holy *mishkan*. Wouldn't you say that Moshe Rabbeinu had many accomplishments to be proud of?"

"Surely, Avi."

"How did he view himself? Did he go about bragging about his accomplishments?"

"Who? Moshe Rabbeinu? The Torah calls him the humblest of all men."

"Precisely, Chaim. With all of his accomplishments, he did not feel that he deserved any privileges or special treatment."

"How do we know that, Avi?"

"This week's *parashah*, Chaim. The first word is 'Vayikra,' which means 'and He called.'"

"Who called to whom, Avi?"

"Hashem called to Moshe. Although Moshe Rabbeinu had many, many accomplishments, which might have earned him special privileges, still he did not enter the innermost chamber of the *mishkan* unless he was summoned by Hashem. This is an example of his great humility."

"It is a good example for us to follow, Avi. I can think of many ways to improve in this area. Speaking softly, not interrupting when someone is speaking, not getting upset when things do not go my way, these are all points to work on."

"Chaim, you are already halfway there. Just realizing that we need to improve is the biggest and most difficult step towards humility."

Simcha's Brain Teaser

You want to send a valuable object to a friend. You have a box which is more than large enough to contain the object. You have several locks with keys. The box has a locking ring which is more than large enough to have a lock attached. But your friend does not have the key to any lock that you have. Note that you cannot send a key in an unlocked box, since it might be copied. How would you do it?

For the answer, turn to the back of the book.

Parashas Tzav

Sacrifice Some Time to Learn about Sacrifices

"Here it is, Chaim, that time of the year again."

"What time, Avi?"

"The time of the year when we learn the Book of Vayikra, the third book of the Chumash."

"You don't sound too excited about it, Avi."

"Chaim, it is such an effort to read the weekly *parashah*."

"Why is that?"

"It's all about korbanos — the offerings brought to the Beis HaMikdash. Two sheep, one cow, two doves, flour, oil, wine, spices, it's all so confusing to me. In the other books of the Chumash, we learn about the lives of our forefathers, or the laws that we need to know for daily living. Korbanos seem far off and unrelated."

"I also felt the same way, Avi, until I started looking into the deeper meanings behind some of the *korbanos*."

"What did you learn, Chaim?"

"I learned about a whole new world that is very exciting and relevant to our lives."

"Really? Can you share it with me?"

"Sure, Avi. Just sit back and close your eyes. We're drifting back in time to the days of the Beis HaMikdash..."

"Shmully, come with me to the flock of sheep."

"Sure thing, Father. What are we going to do there?"

"We're going to pick out a nice, one-year old sheep to be our *korban Pesach*.

"Wow, Father, I almost forgot. Pesach is drawing near."

"That's right, Shmully. This year you are old enough to go with us to the Beis HaMikdash!"

"Really, Father? I'm so excited! I've been looking forward to this my whole life!"

"Now is your chance, Shmully. First, let's pick out our nicest sheep to take with us to Yerushalayim."

After days of packing, the family is ready to make their *aliyah l'regel*, the thrice-annual trip up to Yerushalayim for the holidays of Pesach, Shavuos, and Sukkos.

"Okay, have we packed everything?"

"I think so, Father."

"How about our *korban Pesach*?"

"He's right here."

"Good, let's get going."

"Come sit near me, Shmully. I'll tell you all about what you will see when we get to Yerushalayim."

"Father, there are so many families traveling the roads with us."

"Shmully, all of the Jewish families from all over the Land of

Israel are converging on Yerushalyim to celebrate the festival of Pesach together."

"But Father, isn't that dangerous? Can't enemies attack our borders?"

"Hashem gives the Jewish people special protection this time of year. No danger has ever befallen us as a result of our *aliyah l'regel*. Now, let's review what you learned about the *korban Pesach*, Shmully. First, where and when is it *shechted*?"

"In the courtyard of the Beis HaMikdash, after midday on the eve of Pesach."

"Right."

"Father, how are all of these people, each with their sheep for a *korban Pesach*, going to fit into the courtyard of the Beis HaMikdash in one afternoon?"

"That's a great question, Shmully. When we get to Yerushalayim, you will see miraculous things. Everyone will squeeze into that small area in three shifts. The *kohanim* will work super-fast, doing their part to help each one with his *korban*. The *levi'im* will be singing psalms of praise to Hashem and playing trumpets the entire time."

"Father, I am so excited."

And so it went. Shmully and the family arrived in Yerushalayim and made their preparations for the big day. On the eve of Pesach, they all went to the Beis HaMikdash and were in awe of the miraculous events there.

"Now, Shmully, it's time for us to roast our *korban Pesach*."

"Why do we roast it on the fire instead of cooking it in a pot, Father?"

"Very good question, Shmully. The *korban Pesach*, like the

other mitzvos of the night of Pesach, reminds us that tonight we were freed from slavery in Mitzrayim. We left Mitzrayim very quickly and suddenly. Therefore, we cook the *korban Pesach* in the quickest possible way, which is roasting. We eat the *korban Pesach* like noblemen. Wealthy people roast their meat. Although it shrinks, it is very tasty. Poor people boil meat. Although it does not taste as good, it absorbs water and expands, so there is more meat to eat. But a rich man doesn't worry about having enough to eat. Tonight, we eat like rich men.

"Now, Shmully, when we eat our *korban Pesach*, make sure you do not leave any leftovers. If any meat is left over the next morning, we must burn it."

"Why, Father?"

"Because a rich person knows that he will have enough to eat tomorrow. Therefore, he does not save leftovers. If he leaves over any food, he destroys it and eats fresh food the next day. There is one more thing you must be careful about when eating from the *korban Pesach*, Shmully."

"What's that, Father?"

"Do not break any of the bones while you are eating the meat."

"There are so many rules, Father. How will I remember them all?"

"Don't worry, Shmully. You do your best, and Hashem will help you."

"I'll bet you know what I am going to ask next, Father."

"Let me guess. Why don't we break the bones of the *korban Pesach*?"

"Right, Father!"

"Poor people, who are very hungry, break the bones of the meat and eat the marrow. However, tonight we are noblemen. We would never dream of breaking the bones of the *korban Pesach*."

"Father, now that I have learned so much about the *korban Pesach*, I can't wait to eat it!"

We now drift back to our friends, Chaim and Avi.

"Wow, Chaim! That is so interesting. I never dreamed that *korbanos* could be so fascinating."

"Sure, Avi. You know, we can also have some of the feeling that Shmully had when eating from his *korban Pesach*."

"How's that, Chaim?"

"The *afikoman*, the last piece of matzah that we eat at the seder, represents the *korban Pesach*. When we eat it, we can think of the many ways that it represents freedom. Just like Shmully, we can enjoy the feeling of being free men."

Simcha's Brain Teaser

A truck travels 15 mph for the first half of the distance of a trip. The driver wants to average 30 mph for the whole trip. How fast must he travel for the second half of the trip?

For the answer, turn to the back of the book.

Parashas Shemini

You Are What You Eat

"Hi, Avi! How are you doing?"

"*Baruch Hashem*, Chaim."

"Do you want to come with us to the hospital today?"

"I generally try to avoid hospitals, Chaim."

"I am talking about going to the hospital to do a mitzvah."

"Which mitzvah is that, Chaim?"

"*Bikur cholim*, the mitzvah of visiting the sick, Avi."

"Sure, Chaim. I'll be happy to go. When it comes to doing mitzvos, I'm always ready to lend a helping hand."

While walking down one of the corridors of the hospital, Avi and Chaim overhear the doctors speaking to a woman.

"Mrs. Cohen, the prognosis looks good. Your husband stands a good chance of making a complete recovery."

"*Baruch Hashem*, Dr. Friedman."

"He will have to go on a very strict diet, however. It may be time consuming for you to prepare his special food."

"Whatever you say, doctor. My husband's recovery is more important than anything else."

"He will have to avoid salt, sugar, fried foods, microwaved foods, fats, high cholesterol foods, and dairy products. I will give you a detailed report of precisely what he can and cannot eat before he is ready to leave the hospital."

"Thank you so much, Dr. Friedman."

"Chaim and Avi continue visiting patients in the hospital. A short time later, they overhear the same Dr. Friedman speaking to another woman."

"Mrs. Black, I have some not-so-good news for you."

"Oh no, doctor, what is it?"

"The prognosis does not look very good for your husband."

"But doctor, isn't there anything you can do to help him? Perhaps a special diet?"

"You can try, but I don't think it will make a difference. I am sorry, Mrs. Black."

Chaim and Avi think about the doctor's words.

"The diet will help Mr. Cohen, but not Mr. Black."

"You know, Avi, there is something very important that we can learn from this."

"What is that, Chaim?"

"If you look in this week's Torah portion, *parashas Shemini*, you find two lists of animals. One is a list of kosher animals that are permissible to eat, and the other is a list of non-kosher animals. Why are some foods forbidden to eat? They seem perfectly nutritious and appetizing. The *Midrash Rabba*, a commentary on the Torah written by our great Talmudic Sages, explains with a story. There were two patients: one was going to live, and the other was not. The one who was going to live needed a special diet to nurse him back to health. The other had no hope, so there was no point restricting his diet."

"Chaim, that's just like the two conversations we overheard here in the hospital today."

"Exactly my point, Avi. The Torah puts us on a special diet called '*kashrus*.' It is for our own benefit, to insure a long and productive physical and spiritual life. We're going to live! However, we have to follow the diet, to guard our health."

"You know what they say, Chaim, 'You are what you eat.' Eating kosher is a must for those who strive to learn Torah and keep mitzvos."

"Avi, all of this talk about food is making me hungry."

"Me, too, Chaim. Let's go home and eat a good lunch so we can have more energy to do more mitzvos."

"*B'tei'avon*, Avi."

"What does that mean, Chaim?"

"Have a good appetite!"

Simcha's Brain Teaser

There are three boxes. One is labeled "Apples," another is labeled "Oranges." The last one is labeled "Apples and Oranges." You know that each is labeled incorrectly. You can pick one fruit from any one box which you choose. Which box do you draw from, and how can you label the boxes correctly?

For the answer, turn to the back of the book.

Parashas Tazria

Watch What You Say

C"haim, it's getting late. Time to start getting ready for bed."

"Just a few more minutes, Mommy."

"You've had so much time already, Chaim."

"But I'm doing my math homework, Mommy."

"What's the matter, Chaim? You look upset."

"Mr. Gross, our math teacher, gives us so much homework. He makes it so hard for us. I think he does it on purpose because he doesn't like us."

"Chaim, that's not a very nice thing to say."

"I'll tell you something else. His clothes are not so neat and clean. Sometimes I want to laugh when I look at him. How can someone who is teaching a subject as precise as math, be so sloppy in his appearance?"

"Chaim, I'm sorry but I must stop you from saying anything further. You are speaking *lashon hara*."

"What do you mean *lashon hara*? Everything I've said is 100 percent true."

"That's precisely what *lashon hara* is, Chaim. Any derogatory statement made about another person is *lashon hara*. Even if it is true. If it is not true, it has a different name: *motzi sheim ra*. I had to stop you because you are not allowed to say *lashon hara*, and I am not allowed to listen to it."

"Why is that, Mommy? Mr. Gross will never find out."

"Chaim, I'm sure you have heard of the Chafetz Chaim."

"Sure, Mommy. He was the great rabbi who lived about a hundred years ago. His name was really Rav Yisrael Meir Kagan."

"Do you know how he came to be called the Chafetz Chaim?"

"I always wanted to know, Mommy."

"He wrote a book entitled *Chafetz Chaim*."

"How did he come up with such a name?"

"He named it after a verse in Tehillim (34:13): 'Who is the man who desires life (*chafetz chaim*), who loves days of seeing good? Guard your tongue from evil and your lips from speaking deceit.' Someone who wants to live a long, good life must watch what he says. He must be on guard all of the time. Gossip, deceit, or slander must never cross his lips."

"But I still don't understand how it works, Mommy."

"Every time someone speaks *lashon hara*, he downgrades his fellowman. If the person being spoken about hears it or finds out about it, he will have bad feelings toward the speaker. When others hear the *lashon hara*, it lowers their opinion of the one being spoken about. All of this causes nothing but bad feelings between people.

In the days of the Beis HaMikdash, people who spoke *lashon hara* used to contract a terrible disease called *tzora'as*. This week's *parashah*, *Tazria*, is all about this ailment. The one who had spoken *lashon hara* and was subsequently stricken with *tzora'as*, had to go into isolation until he was cured. That was part of the healing process. When he was all alone, he could not speak any *lashon hara* because there was no one to speak to. Also, he would have time to contemplate and realize that such a severe disease must have been caused by a serious crime."

"Mommy, I never realized that I had to be so careful about my speech. I will surely do my best to never say anything like that about Mr. Gross again. By the way, here is a note that Mr. Gross asked all of the students to give to their parents."

"Mr. Gross is asking all of the parents to come to a special meeting with him tonight."

"Oh, no. He is probably going to scold us for all of the bad things we have been saying about him."

"Let's try to keep a positive attitude, Chaim. Let me make a few phone calls to make arrangements to go to the meeting."

That night, Chaim could not fall asleep because he was worried about the meeting. What terrible things did Mr. Gross have to say about the students who spoke badly about him?

"Mommy, is that you?"

"Chaim, you should have been asleep a long time ago."

"I know, Mommy, but I was worried about the meeting. What did Mr. Gross say?"

"Believe it or not, Chaim, he called the meeting out of concern for the students. He saw that you were having trouble with the new math, so he wanted to explain to the parents how to help the students understand the subject. Now I will be able to help you with your homework."

"Is that all he said, Mommy?"

"No, he also spoke about the class."

"Oh, no. I was afraid of that."

"He praised all of the students in the class for their seriousness and dedication. He said that you are all fine children. He thanked us for giving him the privilege of teaching you."

"You're kidding."

"No, I'm not. Mr. Gross is really a very fine man. *Baruch Hashem* you have such a good teacher."

"Mommy, tomorrow I'm going to go right up to Mr. Gross and tell him how much I appreciate being in his class. I'm going to thank him for being such a caring teacher."

"Chaim, Rav Yisrael Meir, the Chafetz Chaim, would be very proud of you."

Simcha's Brain Teaser

Use the digits 1, 2, 3, 4, 5, and 6 once only, in this multiplication sum to make it correct.

??
x ?
???

For the answer, turn to the back of the book.

Tremendous Power

"Avi, isn't this a great tour?"

"It sure is, Chaim. Where else would we get to see these big looms that weave the fabrics that make up the clothing that we wear?"

"You're right, Avi. Excuse me, Mr. Tour Guide, how many looms are in this factory?"

"Excellent question, young man. We actually have 247 standard looms in this factory. They are all arranged in rows according to the fabric that they make. Some make thick material, some fine, some single-weave, some double-weave, some cotton, some wool, some polyester, and all types of blends."

"Wow, 247 looms is sure a lot, sir."

"I said 247 standard looms. We have one other loom that is not standard."

"Is it bigger or smaller than the standard looms, sir?"

"Let me take you to see it boys. You can judge for yourselves."

With that, the group walked to the far end of the factory. They stood in front of two huge steel sliding doors. Making sure that no one was standing too close to the doors, the tour guide pressed a button and the doors slowly began to slide apart. The boys could not believe their eyes. Standing behind those doors was a monster of a machine. Its tons of high-density stainless steel dwarfed all other machines around it.

"That is some loom, sir."

"It sure is, boys. It is so big and powerful, that it can produce as much fabric as all of the other machines in this factory combined. Look now, the workers are about to fire it up."

The wheels of the giant machine slowly began to turn. The threads slowly began to feed in. Faster and faster the machine accelerated. Within minutes, hundreds of yards of fabric were coming out of the giant loom. The boys practically had to shout to be heard over the noise of the machinery.

"Sir, that is amazing. We have never seen anything quite like that. A machine that can produce so much in so little time."

Suddenly, warning whistles began sounding. The giant loom was malfunctioning. The workers scurried around to turn off the machine, but it was too late. In those few seconds, hundreds of yards of fabric were ruined.

"Boys, now you have seen the other side of it. This machine is wonderful when it is running properly. When it is malfunctioning, however, it will ruin more fabric than all of the other looms combined. We really have to watch this baby. It has tremendous potential, both to create fabric and to destroy it."

"Sir, have you ever heard of the Chafetz Chaim?"

"Did he work in the fabric industry?"

"No, he was the leading rabbi of the Jewish people during the early part of this century. He wrote several books about the mitzvos of proper speech."

"Do you mean pronunciation and grammar?"

"No, he wrote about not degrading other people. He encouraged people to use their gift of speech for only good things, and not to hurt others with words. Sir, you may wonder why I began talking about him."

"That thought did cross my mind, young man."

"In one of his books, the Chafetz Chaim compared the human body to a factory, much the same as yours."

"No kidding."

"Each of the 248 limbs of the body corresponds to one of the 248 positive mitzvos in the Torah."

"Wait a minute, 248 is the number of looms that we have here in our factory."

"Exactly. Each loom can produce material, just as each limb can 'produce' a mitzvah. One limb however, is as powerful as all of the other 247 combined."

"Just like here in the factory. Now you really have my curiosity aroused. Which limb is the most powerful one?"

"It is...the tongue. Our gift of speech, when used properly to study Torah and say nice things about people, can 'produce' more mitzvos than all of the other limbs put together. After all, learning Torah is equal to all of the other mitzvos combined. That is the positive side. However, just as that giant loom has a negative side, so too does the power of speech. When that loom is malfunctioning, it can ruin more material than any other machine. Similarly, when we speak badly, we cause more destruction than with any other limb of our body."

"Boys, that is amazing."

"Thank you very much for the tour, sir. It was very enlightening."

"Boys, I am the one who must thank you. You have enlightened me to the tremendous power of speech. That giant loom will remind me that when I speak properly, I create great things. And there is no greater destructive force than improper speech."

"Sir, we're sure that you will keep the machine running in tip-top shape."

Simcha's Brain Teaser

What number is two-thirds of one-half of one-fourth of 240?

For the answer, turn to the back of the book.

Parashas Acharei Mos

Yearly Cleaning

"Avi, what's in the bag?"

"My nice suit that I wear on Shabbos and Yom Tov. I am taking it to be cleaned and fixed."

"Can I see how it looks?"

"Sure, Chaim."

"Wow, look at all of those stains."

"This is almost a whole year's worth of dropped food, spilled drinks, muddy puddles, and other grime."

"Avi, your suit is ripped over here on the sleeve."

"I know, Chaim. The cleaner is going to send it to a fabric repair place where they can re-weave the cloth and you will never see the tear."

"That's amazing."

"I just hope that they fix it quickly. I love wearing a nice, clean suit on Shabbos and Yom Tov, and especially on Yom Kippur."

"Avi, that is almost poetic."

"In what way, Chaim?"

"Because Yom Kippur is like sending your suit to be cleaned and repaired."

"Chaim, you know that we are not allowed to clean or sew clothes on Yom Kippur."

"Of course, Avi. I am referring to the cleaning and fixing that our souls receive on Yom Kippur."

"Why do our souls need cleaning and fixing?"

"Avi, whenever we make a mistake in a mitzvah or halachah we put a 'stain' on our souls. It is like a little piece of spiritual dirt or a tear in the fabric. Just as our clothing is not so nice when it is stained or torn, so too our souls are not the same. Yom Kippur is a once yearly cleaning and repair of all of the mistakes that have left stains on our souls."

"That's great! How do you know all of this, Chaim?"

"It is in this week's *parashah*, Avi. The beginning of *parashas Acharei Mos* describes the Yom Kippur service in the Beis HaMikdash. In those days, the service was very elaborate, in-

volving sacrifices, incense, and many other things."

"It sounds fascinating, Chaim."

"Come, let's read about it together. The main thing that we need to remember is that Hashem does a wonderful favor for us each year. He allows us to start with a clean, fresh slate. Do you know that good feeling that you have after you wash and put on fresh clothes?"

"Sure, it's great."

"That is what Hashem does for our souls on Yom Kippur."

"Okay, Chaim. I'll see you after I drop this off at the cleaners. I want to learn all about Yom Kippur. Maybe if we learn enough Torah law, we will not make the mistakes in the first place."

"That's the spirit, Avi. Let's put those dry cleaners out of business!"

Simcha's Brain Teaser

Esti is Shoshana's daughter's aunt's husband's daughter's sister. What is the relationship between Esti and Shoshana?

For the answer, turn to the back of the book.

Parashas Kedoshim

Cleaning Up Your Judgment

"That will be thirty shekels, young man."

"When will my suit be ready, sir?"

"About five o'clock."

"Where can I find it?"

"Hanging there on the coatrack in the hallway."

The dry cleaning service is a big convenience for the yeshivah students. The cleaners come to the yeshivah to collect the soiled clothes and return them the same day, fresh and clean. The prices are reasonable. Sometimes it's a bit difficult for the *bachurim* to find their suit among all the others, but if they persevere, they always succeed.

The young man intended to go look for his suit at five o'clock that day. He even told his *chavrusa* to remind him. But they both became so engrossed in their Torah study that they forgot all about the suit.

As he was riding home from the yeshivah, the young man suddenly remembered the suit. For a fleeting moment, he worried. *Oy vey. There are so many people passing through the yeshivah. The doors are not locked. Anyone can come in and take anything they want. I hope my suit will be okay there overnight.* He reassured himself, thinking that there was really nothing to worry about, and continued on his way home. The next morning, the first thing he did upon arriving in yeshivah was to look for his suit.

"Let's see what's hanging on the coatrack. I cannot seem to find my suit. But there are many coatracks in this yeshivah. I'll look on some of the others. Hmmm...still no sign of it."

He spotted the dry-cleaning man who collects the clothes every day. "Excuse me sir, do you remember the suit I dropped off yesterday?"

"I surely do, young man."

"Was it cleaned and brought back?"

"Just a minute, I'll call the cleaners on my cellular phone and check it out... Yes, it was brought back last night a five o'clock. Are you sure you checked all of the coatracks?"

"I guess I'll check again."

With that, the young man looked over the coatracks again. He was now getting very upset. "Someone took my suit," he thought. "It's gone, I'll never find it. Now I have to buy a new suit. What did I do to deserve this?" Frustrated and upset he went to his morning *chavrusa* to apologize for being late.

"I hope you weren't looking for your suit," his *chavrusa* said. "After we finished learning last night, I remembered that you didn't pick it up, so I went to get it. I put it in my dorm room for safe-keeping overnight."

"Thank you so much for thinking about me. You've taught me a real lesson."

By judging others favorably you get a mitzvah. As it is written in this week's *parashah* (Vayikra 19:15), "Judge your fellow Jew righteously." Things are not always as they seem. Take the time to examine your judgment before you jump to conclusions. Perhaps there is a good explanation for this seemingly bad situation. Our friend thought there was some dirty business going on at the dry cleaners. Things turned out to be clean as a whistle.

Simcha's Brain Teaser

Shimon took a job working in a grocery store. For every day he worked, he was paid two dollars. For every day that he was absent, he lost three dollars from his wages. At the end of thirty days, his paycheck was zero. How many days did he work, and how many was he absent?

For the answer, turn to the back of the book.

Count the Days

"Avi, you're still up! It's so late, dear. Why don't you go to sleep?"

"I can't sleep, Mommy. I'm too excited."

"What are you excited about, Avi?"

"My birthday party, Mommy. All of the family will be there, and we'll have such a nice meal with such delicious desserts, and a big birthday cake."

"Just like every year, Avi dear."

"And then I'll get to open the presents."

"Sure."

"Grandma and Grandpa always bring me a beautiful big toy. Books, puzzles, games — I'll be busy for weeks!"

"No wonder you can't sleep."

"Mommy, I've even been counting the days."

"How many days till your birthday, Avi?"

"Eight, not counting today."

"How long have you been counting the days?"

"Two weeks now."

"I can see that for a special event like this, you are so excited that you can't wait for the days to pass."

"Exactly, Mommy. That's why I'm counting them."

"Do you know the Jewish people as a nation collectively count the days together during a certain period of time every year?"

"Are you referring to the counting of the *omer*, Mommy?"

"Yes, I am, Avi. We are anticipating a very special event, much greater than your birthday."

"I know, Mommy. The giving of the Torah on Har Sinai."

"That's right, Avi. The Torah is Hashem's greatest gift to mankind. It is the blueprint for the world and the guide for our lives. Without the Torah, none of us would be here."

"Really, Mommy?"

"Yes, Avi. Hashem has preserved and guarded the Jewish people all of these thousands of years because we have preserved and guarded His Torah. There is no greater gift. Not only that, Torah study is very enjoyable. One who learns Torah finds it sweeter than honey. This year, like every year, on the holiday of Shavuos, we celebrate the giving of the Torah on Har Sinai. If we prepare ourselves properly for the reception of this great gift, we will be able to receive it in its entirety, just as our ancestors did 3300 years ago."

"Really, Mommy?"

"Yes, Avi. That is Hashem's gift to us. Therefore, we count the days. Every day another preparation. Every day another step closer. Day by day, we count our steps as we draw closer and closer to the big event."

"Mommy, you've gotten me so excited about Shavuos that I'll never fall asleep!"

"Don't worry, Avi. Lay in bed, relax, and think about all of the good that Hashem has done for you. You'll be asleep in no time."

Simcha's Brain Teaser

Which year of the twentieth century reads the same if you turn it upside down?

For the answer, turn to the back of the book.

He's Taking Care of Us

C haim, you're not going to believe this."

"Believe what, Avi?"

"Believe what my teacher taught us today about the *shemittah* year."

"Is that the year where the farmer is forbidden to work the land?"

"Correct, Chaim. One in every seven years the land is allowed to rest."

"What's so unbelievable about that? Crop rotation is supposed to be a good thing."

"My teacher quoted the great Rav Chaim Shmuelevitz, the late head of the yeshivah in Mir, Poland."

"What did he say?"

"Those who observed the *shemittah* year were like heavenly angels. Their strength was unfathomable. How can it be that a person can achieve such great things from the mitzvah of *shemittah*?"

"Let's think about this a minute, Avi. Let us try to imagine ourselves back in the days of the Beis HaMikdash..."

"Father, thank you so much for taking such good care of us. *Baruch Hashem*, we have a nice farm, and every day you go out and work the fields. You plow, plant, and tend to the crops. When they are grown, you pick them and bring them to Mother to cook into the delicious meals that we eat. We are so fortunate that we have such a farm and that it is able to provide food for our family."

"Children, do you know what next year is?"

"What, Father?"

"The *shemittah* year. Next year I take a big vacation. No plowing, planting, cultivating, or working the land. We will see what will grow by itself. Even those crops are not ours. They are *hefker* and free for anyone to take."

"But Father, what will we have to eat next year? If you do not work the land, and anyone can take what grows by itself, we will have hardly any food."

"Children, the Torah asks the exact same question in Vayikra (25:20). The answer is that Hashem will provide for us. This year He will give us enough food to last until after the *shemittah* year."

"And so it was, Avi. There are no records of any famine ever occurring amongst the Jewish people in Biblical times as a result of keeping the *shemittah* year. In the times of the Beis HaMikdash, farming was the main occupation of the Jewish people. Without the crops of the farm, there would be literally no food to eat. Observing the *shemittah* was therefore a very big test of one's trust in Hashem. That is why Rav Chaim Shmuelevitz says that those who observed *shemittah* are compared to heavenly angels who have no desire to go against Hashem's will. That is the strength of their trust in Him."

Simcha's Brain Teaser

A woman has planted some flowers of three different kinds. There are roses, tulips, and daisies. How many flowers do I have if all of them are roses except two, all of them are tulips except two, and all of them are daisies except two.

For the answer, turn to the back of the book.

Toiling

Chaim, hurry. You don't want to be late for school."
"I'm watching these construction workers, Avi. It's fascinating. Those three over there are working very slowly. However, that one on the left is working twice as fast as they are. Look at him go."

"You're right, Chaim, but we also have to work fast if we want to get to school on time."

"I will catch up to you, Avi. But I just want to ask that fast worker a few questions."

"Okay, Chaim. I hope you make it."

"Excuse me, sir. I do not want to disturb you because I see that you are working so hard. I just want to ask you something."

"Go ahead, young man."

"I see that you are working twice as fast as these other workers. Why is that? Don't you want to take it easy?"

"That is a good question, young man. I will explain the situation to you. Our boss pays us for the amount of work that we do. If we can accomplish more in the same amount of time, we will make more money. God has blessed my wife and I with a big family. We have many expenses, so I need to make enough money to pay the bills. Therefore I must work very hard to produce more and earn more money. Those other men do not have such big families, so they do not need so much money. Therefore, they can be a little more relaxed in their work. "

"Now I understand, sir. Thank you very much for taking some of your precious time to answer my question."

"Not at all, young man. I feel very good about my work. When I begin to work in the morning, I think that I am doing my job in order to feed and clothe my wife and children. That motivates me to work as hard as I can. I enjoy my work very much because I know what good things it produces."

"Bye-bye, sir. I have to go to school now. That is my job. I don't want to be late."

Chaim hurries to school and arrives just as the morning bell sounds. The first class of the day is *parashas hashavua*.

"Okay, boys. Let us begin this week's Torah portion, *parashas Bechukosai*. Chaim, will you please read first?"

"Yes, Rabbi Lebowitz. 'If you will follow My decrees and observe My commandments and perform them.' "

"Very good, Chaim. Now please read Rashi's commentary on the words 'and observe My commandments.' "

" 'You should toil in the study of Torah in order to guard and fulfill [the mitzvos].' "

"Excellent, Chaim. Can anyone explain what this means?"

"I believe that I can, Rabbi Lebowitz."

"Go right ahead, Chaim."

"This morning on the way to school I saw a construction worker who was toiling away at his job. I asked him why he was working so hard. He explained to me that he had a big family and many expenses, therefore he needed to work hard to earn the money to pay the bills. He said that he felt good knowing that his work helped to feed and clothe his family. That motivated him to work very hard."

"Very good, Chaim. How do we apply that to toiling in Torah? What is our motivation?"

"When we learn Torah, we are doing a mitzvah that is equal to all of the other mitzvos combined."

"Excellent, Chaim. What is the source for that?"

"The end of the *mishnah* in *Peah* that we say after our *birkas haTorah* every morning: 'Vetalmud Torah keneged kulam' — Learning Torah is equal to all the mitzvos."

"Chaim, you are a real, budding *talmid chacham*."

"May I add something, Rabbi Lebowitz?"

"Yes, Avi."

"Our Torah learning provides the spiritual energy that keeps the world running."

"Wonderful, Avi. When we sit down to learn Torah, let us all think about that construction worker that Chaim saw this morning. If supporting his family makes him toil so hard, then how much more so should we toil. We are supporting much more than one family. We are supporting the entire world. If the construction worker is happy and satisfied knowing that his work supports his family, how much more so should we be happy and satisfied knowing that we are supporting the world."

"Thank you so much, Rabbi Lebowitz!"

"You're welcome, boys! Now, who will read the next verse? We must get to work here. The world is depending on us."

Everyone begins to read at once. " 'Then I will provide your rains in their time...' "

"Boys, your toiling is music to my ears."

Simcha's Brain Teaser

If you were to put a coin into an empty bottle and then insert a cork into the neck, how could you remove the coin without taking out the cork or breaking the bottle?

For the answer, turn to the back of the book.

Bemidbar

The Organization Man

"Avi, how are you?"

"Great, Chaim. How are you?"

"Fine, *baruch Hashem*. I'm on my way to play baseball. Do you want to come?"

"I'd really like to, Chaim, but I can't right now. I have to straighten up and reorganize my room."

"I'm sure that can wait, Avi. The ball game won't take that long."

"Unfortunately, it can't wait, Chaim. My room has been a mess for a long time. It is getting harder and harder to find things in the drawers and closets. I waste so much time looking for my belongings. I have to straighten it out once and for all. Once I do that, I'll have much more time for baseball, and everything else."

"I guess I understand, Avi. I just never thought that being organized was that important."

"Really? Just take a look at this week's *parashah*, Chaim. Do you see how much time and effort the Torah takes to explain the way the Jewish people camped and traveled in the desert?"

"What do you mean, Avi?"

"In *parashas Bemidbar*, you will find a detailed description of the encampment of the Jewish people: which tribe camped to the north, south, center, etc. The Torah then relates the job description of those *levi'im* who assembled and carried the *mishkan*. The next *parashah* depicts exactly how they would break camp: who would travel first, and so on, until the last tribe to travel. Do you realize how much time and effort go into relating these details to us?"

"I never thought about it, Avi."

"We all know that the Torah does not waste a single word or letter. Therefore, there must be a tremendous significance in all of this information."

"What is it, Avi?"

"Rabbi Aharon Kotler, of blessed memory, the founder of the Lakewood Yeshivah, answers this question. The Torah is teaching us the importance of organization. On a simple level, order saves time. Time is our most precious possession, something which cannot be replaced. When a moment is lost, we can never retrieve it. We can use all of our time productively if we are prepared and organized. Time is also lost looking for objects which are misplaced. So we see, Chaim, that organization and time are intimately related."

"Wow."

"But there's even more to it. Rabbi Kotler relates order to holiness. Just think about the mitzvos that we do. Each one has specific instructions that must be performed in a particular sequence. Without that order, the mitzvah is lost. Our prayers are all arranged in a beautiful symphony of psalms and praises to Hashem, one flowing into the next. Mitzvos, and the holiness they impart, are impossible without *seder*. Now do you see why I must organize my room right away, Chaim?"

"I sure do, Avi. You have opened my eyes to a whole new way of thinking. Being organized and prioritized is a lot more important than I ever thought."

"Now you've got your priorities right, Chaim!"

Simcha's Brain Teaser

Sarah helped her mother put the socks away yesterday. She put them in the drawer, but did not pair them. Sarah's father had six black socks, four blue socks, and eight colored socks. He got up early the next day to study Torah. He did not want to turn the light on and wake up his wife. He needed two socks that matched, but he could not see anything in the drawer. What is the smallest number of socks that he had to pull out of the drawer to get a matching pair?

For the answer, turn to the back of the book.

Parashas Naso

Shalom

C haim, is *shalom* a good thing?"

"It sure is, Avi."

"How good is it?"

"It's better than ice cream and cake."

"Let's be serious, Chaim."

"I am serious. I would not fight over a piece of cake."

"I see what you mean. Do you know how much the Torah values *shalom*?"

"Let's see. We greet each other with *shalom*. We also bid each other farewell with *shalom*. It must be important. We also learn about Aharon HaCohen, the brother of Moshe Rabbeinu. The Torah praises him because he loved *shalom* and pursued it."

"Chaim, I never thought of that. I'll tell you what I was thinking. I was reading the *midrash* on this week's *parashah*. The subject was the blessings of the *kohanim*. The last blessing is 'May Hashem shine His face upon you and grant you peace.' The *midrash* lists twenty reasons why *shalom* is great."

"Really, Avi? Twenty reasons?"

"That's right, Chaim. Then it lists eight reasons why *shalom* is so dear to us."

"Twenty reasons why *shalom* is great. Wow! Can you tell me one?"

"Sure, Chaim. *Shalom* is equal in value to everything else in the world put together. We see this reflected in our morning prayers. 'Hashem forms light and dark, makes peace and creates everything.' First He must make peace. Then He can create everything. Peace is the foundation upon which everything is created."

"That's great, Avi! Tell me another reason why peace is so great."

"Okay, Chaim. Idol worship is one of the worst sins. Yet if there is *shalom* among the Jewish people, Hashem will not punish them severely for idol worship. Can you imagine that? *Shalom* can fend off the worst punishment."

"More, Avi. I want to hear more."

"Do you want to receive the blessings of wisdom, health, wealth, and children, Chaim?"

"Of course I do, Avi."

"*Shalom* is the best container for blessing. Nothing holds blessings better than *shalom*. It's better than aluminum foil, Saran wrap, and Ziplock bags all put together. Our daily prayers end with the blessing for peace. The priestly blessings end with the blessing for peace. We quote a verse from Tehillim in our daily prayers, 'Hashem blesses His nation with peace.' "

"Avi, I never realized..."

"Chaim, we have a mighty power at our fingertips. With it we can reap untold blessings. We can avoid punishment. We can acquire something as valuable as the world itself! That is the power of *shalom.*"

"Avi, I am really going to work on increasing *shalom* in the world. I am going to think twice before getting upset. I am going to try to have more patience. I am going to stay as far away from argument as I possibly can. *Shalom* is a great thing. A real treasure."

"Chaim, sometimes the biggest treasure is buried right in your own backyard. Come, let's go tell some of the guys."

"Avi, I'm with you all the way."

"Shalom, Mendy! How are you?"

"Shalom, shalom Yaakov, good to see you! Boy do we have something great to tell you."

Simcha's Brain Teaser

A word I know,
six letters it contains,
subtract just one,
and twelve is what remains.

* * *

Pronounced as one letter,
and written with three,
two letters there are,
and two only in me.
I'm double, I'm single,
I'm black, blue, and gray,
I'm read from both ends,
and the same either way.

For the answers, turn to the back of the book.

Basic Training

"Hup, two, three, four! Hup, two, three, four!"

"About face!"

"Left face!"

"Right face!"

"Forward march!"

"Hup, two, three, four!"

"Okay, you guys, tomorrow we're getting up at 5 A.M. for a twenty-mile hike with a twenty-pound backpack. You're in the army now!"

"Dis-missed!"

"What did you learn about in class today, Avi?"

"Funny that you should ask, Chaim. Today we learned about soldiers and the army. Basic training in the army is very rough. They train the soldiers to take orders from their superiors."

"Avi, our ancestors underwent their own basic training in the desert before they entered Eretz Yisrael. They camped in tents for forty years. They traveled from place to place, never knowing their schedule or destination. Hashem guided them each step of the way. They learned to listen to His instructions. After that, observing the commandments was much easier. Try to imagine what it was like, over three thousand years ago in the desert..."

"Here we are in the desert, packing up camp again, getting ready to travel. This is a lot of work, packing up all of our belongings and placing them onto our wagons, donkeys, and camels. The cloud rose up from its place on top of the *mishkan*. That is our sign from Hashem to break camp. We will keep traveling in the direction of the cloud until it comes to rest upon the *mishkan* again."

"We have arrived after a long journey. The cloud has settled, signaling that this is our new encampment. Unpacking is a lot of work, but we will be able to rest when we are settled. This seems to be a very nice place to camp."

"Look at that, the cloud has risen again after only one day! Time to pack up again. This is not easy. I was hoping that we would be staying for a longer time."

"We have reached our destination. This place is actually not so nice. I hope we do not stay too long. Should we unpack everything? Perhaps we are we only going to stay for a short time."

"The cloud has settled down. It has not moved for quite a long time. This traveling has taught me a lesson. Hashem is guiding us. We each have our own ideas about where and when we should travel. However, we travel according to Hashem's wishes."

"Chaim, that's amazing. Now I understand a little better why the Jewish people had the discipline to observe the mitzvos for over three thousand years through all kinds of trials and tribulations. Discipline is something that you have to work hard to acquire. They had a great basic training course in the desert."

"And don't forget their superior officer, Avi. The Almighty got the point across better than any drill sergeant in history. He never even had to say "Hup, two, three, four!"

Simcha's Brain Teaser

A camel has 3000 bananas. He wants to go over a one thousand mile stretch of the desert. He has to eat one banana for each mile he walks. But he can only carry 1000 bananas at a time. Waiting for him on the other side is his family. He wants to find a way to bring as many bananas to them as possible. Hint: He doesn't have to go all the way at once, and he can leave bananas in the desert because he and his camel family are the only camels that eat bananas. Can he bring any bananas to his family? If so, how many?

For the answer, turn to the back of the book.

Everyone's Doing It

Hi everybody, I'm home!"

"Hi Daddy! How was your day at the office?"

"Tiring. It's great to be home with the family. How is everyone feeling?"

"Good, Daddy."

"Thank you so much for the cold drink, Chani. And thank you for hanging up my jacket, Yossie."

"My hard-working husband, Shlomo, how are you?"

"Fine, dear. It warms my heart to see your smiling face after a long day at the office. Where's Avi?"

"We have to talk about that when you have the time, dear."

"How about after dinner?"

"Great."

"Everyone come into the dining room! Let's all sit down and eat the delicious dinner that Mommy worked so hard to prepare."

Later that evening, after dinner, Mom and Dad get a chance to chat.

"What's doing with Avi, dear. He's not himself."

"We had a little disagreement today. He wanted to go swimming in the river with his friend Jerry and some other boys whose names I didn't recognize. I said that swimming in the river is dangerous, and besides that, I did not know any of the boys that were going except for Jerry. I did not let him go."

"What did he say?"

"He wasn't too happy about that. He wanted to know why we were so strict, especially because everybody's parents let them swim in the river. I told him that you would have a talk with him when you came home."

"Okay, dear. You did the right thing. Let's call Avi in here and we'll talk with him together."

"Avi!"

"Yes, Mommy."

"Can you please come into the living room? Daddy and I want to have a little chat with you about what happened today."

"Okay, Mommy."

And so Avi's father begins speaking. "Avi, what is this week's *parashah*?"

"*Parashas Shelach*."

"Do you know how *parashas Shelach* is related to swimming in the river?"

"It's hard to see the connection. There were no rivers in the desert."

"Correct, Avi. The Jewish people were preparing to enter Eretz Yisrael. Hashem had promised them an easy conquest of the land. Moshe Rabbeinu sent twelve men to spy out the land before beginning the battle. They were men of integrity, learned in Torah, the distinguished leaders of the Jewish people and of their respective tribes. Throughout their forty-day mission, they traveled together across the land of Canaan, all seeing the same sights. They returned, however, with varying reports. Ten of them claimed it was a land of giants too powerful to overcome, a land that devoured its inhabitants. Hysteria erupted among the Jewish people. Calev ben Yefunneh tried to silence the people and speak praises of the land.

"Avi, if you were there, how would you react? The respected leaders of the nation, along with the overwhelming majority of the people, are following a report which contradicts the promise that Hashem made to the Jewish people. We know they are wrong, but everyone is following them. Everyone except Calev ben Yefuneh. For this act of standing up for the truth, 'having a different spirit with him,' Hashem refers to him endearingly as 'My servant, Calev' (Bemidbar 14:24). Rav Shimshon Rafael Hirsch explains 'a different spirit' to mean a different understanding, and a different desire, which saved him from the sin of the spies. Calev followed the word of Hashem, even when all were against him."

"Wow, Daddy. That's really exciting. But what does it have to do with swimming in the river?"

"Avi, swimming in a river like that is dangerous. There are undercurrents, jagged rocks, and very deep spots. There are no lifeguards. We do not know any of the boys that went except for Jerry. Under those circumstances, Mommy could not let you go, and I agree with her."

"But Daddy, everyone goes swimming in the river."

"The fact that everyone is doing it does not make it right. Avi, you are not everyone. This time, you have to be different. Just like Calev ben Yefuneh. He was not afraid to go against everyone when he knew that he was right. He didn't follow the crowd."

"You know, Daddy, it's not easy to say no when everyone is going."

"I know, Avi. But the reward is great. Look at Calev's reward. He became close to Hashem Himself."

"Wow, Daddy. You're right. You are my parents and it is my privilege to follow your word. I'm going to be like Calev ben Yefuneh."

"Avi, you make us very, very proud of you."

Simcha's Brain Teaser

Two boys on bicycles, 20 miles apart, began racing toward each other. The instant they started, a fly on the handlebar of one of the bikes started flying toward the other bike's handlebar. As soon as it reached it, it turned around and went to the other bike, and so on until the bikes met. If each bike had a constant speed of 10 mph, and the fly was traveling 15 mph constantly, how far did the fly travel?

For the answer, turn to the back of the book.

Sounds Good to Me

"Avi, are you coming with me to buy an *esrog*?"

"You bet, Chaim. The *esrog* is part of such an important mitzvah, I wouldn't miss out."

"Come, let's go."

"Wow, Avi! Look at this selection of *esrogim*. There are so many beautiful ones!"

"I see, Chaim. This is going to be great fun picking one out. Let's ask the storekeeper to help us. I am sure that he knows all of the halachos of *esrogim*."

"Sir, can you please help us pick out our *esrogim*?"

"Of course I can, boys. Let's step over here and find an especially beautiful one for you."

"Avi, I have mine all picked out. How about you?"

"I have it narrowed down to two. Let's ask how much they cost. Maybe that will help me make up my mind. Excuse me, sir."

"Yes, young man."

"I would like to know how much these *esrogim* cost."

"Let me see them, young man. The one in your left hand is

fifty dollars. The one in your right hand is a little less costly. It is only forty-five dollars."

"Fifty dollars? For one fruit? That is a lot of money! How can it be?"

"The Torah instructs us to take the fruit of a beautiful tree, which we know is the *esrog*. Although the *esrog* tree produces many fruits, very, very few of them meet the halachic requirements of the holiday of Sukkos. It takes much care and work to bring them to the market. That is why they are so expensive."

"You know, sir, this *esrog* looks almost like a lemon. A lemon is the fruit of a beautiful tree. Why can't I use a lemon on Sukkos? I can buy a whole pound of lemons for a dollar."

"Young man, our Rabbis have instructed us that the only fruit which is kosher for this mitzvah is the *esrog*. Other fruits may be very beautiful, but they cannot be used."

"That is a little hard for me to accept."

"Young man, let me tell you about a man who lived a long time ago. His name was Korach. He lived during the time of Moshe Rabbeinu. In reality, he was jealous of Moshe Rabbeinu's position of leadership of the Jewish people. He cloaked this jealousy in the guise of an argument about a Torah law. A garment needs one blue thread in its tzitzis to fulfill its halachic requirements. Therefore, surely a garment made entirely of blue thread does not need tzitzis! This was the 'question' that Korach posed to Moshe Rabbeinu. You see, he was the first Jew to attempt to rewrite the halachah to suit his own needs: 'I don't like the way the Rabbis interpret the Torah. I will interpret it differently. It sounds good to me.'

"So you see, young man, the Rabbis know far more than we

do, and it is ultimately their job to teach us how the interpret the Torah. We cannot change the halachah solely on the basis of our own opinion."

"Thank you so much for explaining that to me, sir. Do you know why the lemon looked more beautiful to me than the *esrog* did?"

"Why, young man?"

"Because I was not wearing my 'halachic eyeglasses.' "

"Sounds good to me."

Simcha's Brain Teaser

Imagine a large empty bin. Each minute people came and put in one *esrog* each. The first minute (starting at 12 noon), one person came and put in one *esrog*. The second minute, two people put in one *esrog* each. A minute later, four people put in one *esrog* each. This pattern continued until the bin was exactly full at 6 P.M. At what time was the bin half empty?

For the answer, turn to the back of the book.

Parashas Chukas

Giant Reward

Og, Melech HaBashan. Og, Melech HaBashan. Og, Melech HaBashan.

"What is that, Chaim, some kind of new breakfast cereal?"

"Not exactly, Avi. Og, Melech HaBashan was a king who lived a very long time. He was alive in the times of Avraham Avinu and did not die until the days of Moshe Rabbeinu, five hundred years later! That's longevity."

"How did he do it, Chaim? Special diet? Exercise? Lots of fresh air?"

"Not exactly, Avi. I'll tell you something else about him that will make your hair stand on end."

"What's that, Chaim?"

"The Jewish people were afraid of him. He heard of their miraculous victories and conquests on the way to Eretz Yisrael after their forty years of wandering in the desert. He went out to battle them. Even though Hashem had promised them Eretz Yisrael, and they had experienced one miracle after another en route to the land, still they were afraid that he might wipe them all out."

"What did he have going for him, Chaim, that struck such

fear into the heart of the people?"

"He had the merit of one mitzvah."

"You're kidding."

"No, I'm not, Avi."

"What was that one mitzvah? It must have been a doozy."

"In the days of Avraham Avinu there was a huge war among nine kingdoms. During that war, Avraham's nephew Lot was captured. Og was one of the survivors of that war. He was jealous of Avraham Avinu and wanted to marry his beautiful wife, Sarah. So he reported to Avraham that Lot had been captured. Og hoped that Avraham would go to war to free Lot and be slain in battle. Then Og could marry Sarah. His plans were foiled when Avraham Avinu succeeded in freeing Lot. Og's mitzvah was informing Avraham of Lot's capture. That enabled Avraham to save him."

"What kind of a mitzvah is that, Chaim? He didn't want

Avraham to save Lot. He wanted Avraham to get killed!"

"You are 100 percent right. He did a mitzvah with absolutely no good intentions. Still, Hashem rewarded him with long life. The merit of that mitzvah was so great, that the Jewish people were afraid he would outlive them and wipe them off the face of the earth."

"I never realized that a mitzvah could be so powerful. Five hundred years of life for one mitzvah. Amazing."

"Where are you going now, Avi?"

"I'm going to look for a mitzvah to do! I don't want to pass a single one by. There are big profits in the Mitzvah Business."

"Avi, you are a smart businessman. I'd like to be your partner."

"Come, let's go learn Torah. That's a great mitzvah!"

"I can feel the stock market rising already."

Simcha's Brain Teaser

You bought a ten-gallon hat as a souvenir of a visit to Texas. When you get home you discover that the label states it is only a six-gallon hat. By now, you are skeptical that it is even that big, and you decide to test it by trying to fill it with six gallons of water. The only containers you have on hand are those listed below. Using them, how are you able to pour six gallons into the hat?

Container A: 9 gallons
Container B: 4 gallons

For the answer, turn to the back of the book.

Parashas Balak

The Ultimate Weapon

Sir, the enemy is advancing at an alarming rate!"

"Repel them with machine gun fire."

"Will do, sir!"

A short time later...

"Sir, the machine gun fire didn't slow them down one bit."

"Try light artillery and hand grenades."

"Yes, sir!"

A short time later...

"Sir, the enemy is still advancing!"

"Fire the heavy artillery at them. We've got to stop them at all costs!"

"Yes sir!"

A short time later...

"Sir, what shall we do? Not even the heavy artillery is slowing them down!"

"Get me the General on the phone.

"General, we're in a tough situation here. We've tried stopping the enemy with everything we have. Nothing is working. What? Are you sure? Yes, sir! No, sir! Yes, sir!"

"What did the General say?"

"He said to use missiles, helicopters, and tanks."

"That will surely stop the enemy."

A short time later...

"Sir, I have terrible news."

"Please, don't tell me."

"The missiles, helicopters, and tanks did absolutely nothing to stop the enemy."

"Oh no! I hate to do this, but I'll have to call the General again.

"Hello, General? The enemy is still advancing. We are desperate. What are our orders, sir? You're going to do what? Yes, sir! Of course, sir! No, sir! Bye, sir!"

"What did the General say?"

"He is going to call the President."

"The P-P-P-President?"

"Yes, the situation is that desperate."

At the President's office...

"Hello. Yes, General. How are you? How is the battle going? Really. Oh no. That's terrible. What are our options? What? Only one option left? There must be something else that we can try. Nothing else? I have to think this one over very carefully. Thank you very much, General. Bye."

"Mr. President, what will we do?"

"We have only one option."

"Oh no! Not the..."

"Yes. We have to press...The Button."

"Oh no, not...The Button. But think of the consequences sir.

Mass destruction, collateral damage, fallout, pain, suffering, disease. Don't we have any other option?"

"I'm afraid not. Bring me The Button."

"But, sir..."

"*Bring it to me!*"

"Yes, sir. Here it is."

"I am now pressing The Button."

A telephone emerges from the box and automatically dials a number...

"Hello."

"Yes, is this the Bilaam residence?"

"Yes."

"This is the President calling. I have a mission for you."

"You know, sir, that my price is very high."

"We will pay whatever you ask. We are desperate."

"Go ahead, Mr. President."

"The enemy is advancing and we cannot stop him. We want you to curse our enemy."

"Send over the Vice President, Secretary of State, Speaker of the House, Joint Chief of Staff, and a whole house filled with silver and gold, and I will come with you to curse your enemy."

"You ask a lot, but we will do it. We're on our way."

"Good-bye, Mr. President."

The President's aid listens in amazement.

"Sir, that's what happens when you press the button?"

"Of course, what did you think?"

"I thought it was the atomic bomb."

"What? The atomic bomb? That's child's play compared to the destructive power of the spoken word. Words have caused more death, destruction, and suffering than all of the atomic bombs in the world put together. And Bilaam is a master of the word. Whomever he blesses is blessed, and whomever he curses is..."

"Wiped out."

"Exactly."

"Now call the General back and tell him that there is nothing to worry about. But make sure you watch what you say. One wrong word and..."

"I know. I see now that the spoken word is the ultimate weapon."

"Let's use it for good."

Simcha's Brain Teaser

A gentleman who passed away recently left just under $8000 to be divided between his widow, his five sons, and his four daughters. He stipulated that every son should receive three times as much as a daughter, and that every daughter should receive twice as much as their mother. If the precise amount left by the man was $7999.97, how much did the widow receive?

For the answer, turn to the back of the book.

Parashas Pinchas

The Spirit of Leadership

O kay, let's choose up sides for the baseball game."

"Who are going to be the team captains?"

"Shlomie, you can be the captain of our team, and Chaim, you will be in charge of the other team."

"Okay, I'll take Yitzy."

"I'll take Yossie."

After all of the players are chosen...

"Okay, who's on first?"

"I want to play first!"

"No, I do!"

"Hmmm. How about second? Any volunteers?"

None.

"How about center field?"

"Me!"

"Me!"

"I want it!"

"How about right field? Nobody? Listen guys, we're going to have to agree on the positions here. Some of you will have to give in."

"Why should I give in? Let him give in!"

"Hmmm. I see that some people have some very strong opinions here. It is not going to be easy to be captain of this team."

"You think this is difficult? This is nothing compared to Yehoshua bin Nun's job."

"Yehoshua bin who? What team did he play for? The Phillies? Wasn't he the pitcher who won twenty games?"

"No, you've got it all wrong. Yehoshua bin Nun was the man chosen to be the leader of the Jewish people after Moshe Rabbeinu. Hashem Himself handpicked Yehoshua."

"Really? What were Yehoshua's leadership qualities?"

"He is described as 'a man who has spirit in him.' "

"What does that mean?"

"Rashi explains that each person had his unique spirit, a unique point of view. A leader needs the patience to relate to each individual person. The other person does not necessarily think the same way that I think. He may not like the same things that I like. Our *gedolim* are all truly great people who have developed the patience to understand people as individuals, to get along with each one and respect his individual preferences. They have the spirit to handle the individual spirits of the people. It begins with little things. This one prefers chocolate, this one vanilla; one likes the front seat, one the back; one likes the window open, the other wants it closed. Yehoshua bin Nun was able to get along with everyone. That is why he became the leader."

"Okay guys, let's try this again. Does this team have spirit?"

"*It sure does!*"

"Is this team going to play its best?"

"*It sure is!*"

"Then this team has to get together and decide on field positions and a batting order."

"*No problem!* You're the captain. Tell us what to do. We'll follow your orders. This team has real spirit! That's because the team captain has real spirit!"

Simcha's Brain Teaser

What is the easiest way to throw a ball, and have it stop, and completely reverse direction after traveling a short distance?

For the answer, turn to the back of the book.

Finish What You Start

A vi."

"Yes, Mommy."

"Please finish your breakfast before you leave for school."

"Yes, Mommy."

Later that day...

"Mommy, can I go out to ride my bicycle now?"

"Did you finish your homework yet, Avi?"

"No, not yet."

"Finish your homework, then you can go out to ride."

The next day at the store...

"Mommy, can you please buy me that model car? It looks so neat and all I have to do is glue it together."

"Avi, did you finish gluing together the last model that I bought you?"

"Uh, no Mommy. Not yet."

"Well, Avi, you have to finish that one first before we can buy you a new one."

"Mommy, it seems that you are always telling me to finish things. Finish your breakfast...finish your homework...finish your model. Why is it so important to finish everything?"

"Avi, dear, may I answer your question with a question?"

"Why not, Mommy?"

"What if Hashem Himself told you to finish something that you started, would you listen to Him?"

"Of course, Mommy."

"That is exactly what happened in the desert, 3300 years ago."

"Really?"

"Yes. Let me tell you the story. The nation of Midian tried to bring about the downfall of the Jewish people. They actually succeeded in convincing one of our leaders to join their way of thinking."

"That's terrible."

"It was actually worse than that. Some of the Jewish people were ready to follow this leader. He was gaining power and a following, and nobody arose to challenge him. The situation was getting worse by the moment. Then Pinchas stepped in. He began the rebellion against the nation of Midian and against the people who were following them."

"What does that have to do with finishing what you start, Mommy?"

"I haven't finished the story yet, Avi. Pinchas began the rebellion but unfortunately, there was no way to avoid a war with the nation of Midian. When it came time to fight the war, Hashem Himself told Pinchas to lead the nation in battle. Normally this would have been the job of the *kohen gadol*, Elazar HaKohen, who was Pinchas' father."

"Why did Pinchas lead the battle and not his father Elazar?"

"Rashi explains the answer to your question, Avi, dear. Pinchas began the rebellion against Midian; therefore, it was his job to finish what he started. We learn from this the importance of finishing what you start."

"Wow, Mommy."

"If you want to get a little philosophical, Avi, think about this. The whole is greater than the sum of the parts. A whole chair is

more than the wood, fabric, and screws that went into making it. You cannot sit comfortably on pieces of wood. A car is much more than the parts that it is made of. They cannot drive you from place to place. Anything, when completed, becomes more than its individual parts. This is especially true of mitzvos. You may put a lot of effort into starting something and getting halfway through. It will take just as much effort to finish. However, you will have a whole thing. A whole complete nutritious meal, a complete homework assignment, a complete project. These are really worth something."

"Thank you so much, Mommy, for finishing the story. You have really inspired me to always try to finish what I start."

"That's a good start, Avi. Keep going and you will finish."

Simcha's Brain Teaser

There are three black hats and two white hats in a box. Three men (we will call them A, B, C,) each reach into the box and place one of the hats on his own head. They cannot see what color hat they have chosen. The men are sitting in a row, with C in front, B in the middle and A at the back, in such a way that A can see the hats on B and C's heads, B can only see the hat on C's head and C cannot see any hats.

When A is asked if he knows the color of the hat he is wearing, he says no. When B is asked if he knows the color of the hat he is wearing, he says no. When C is asked if he knows the color of the hat he is wearing, he says yes, and he is correct.

What color hat is C wearing, and how does he know?

For the answer, turn to the back of the book.

Parashas Masei

Life's Journey

"Chaim, where have you been? I haven't seen you for two weeks."

"My family went on vacation, Avi."

"That sounds great. Where did you go?"

"We took an auto trip down the East Coast. We started from northern Maine and drove all the way down to South Florida, stopping and seeing all of the sights along the way."

"It sounds like an action-packed vacation, Chaim."

"It was, Avi. The whole family was together and we all have lots of good memories."

"Family memories are a great thing. Years from now, you can look back on them."

"I have this road map of our itinerary. It reminds me of all of the places that we visited."

" 'These are the journeys of Chaim's family.' "

"Ha ha. You sound like you are quoting this week's *parashah*. It begins with the words, 'These are the journeys of the Children of Israel.' "

"I am quoting it, Chaim. The Torah lists all of the encamp-

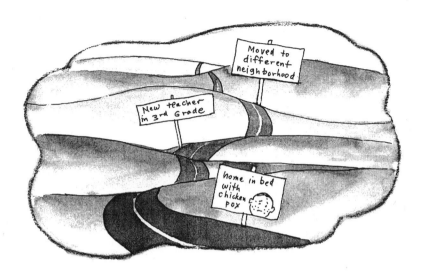

ments of the Jewish people during the forty years of wandering in the desert."

"I always wondered about that, Avi. Why did the Torah take the trouble to make such a complete list? These places have already been mentioned earlier in the Torah. We all know that the Torah does not waste words."

"Excellent question, Chaim! The great Bible commentator Rabbeinu Bechayei answers your question. He explains that Hashem wanted to strengthen the faith of the Jewish people. Therefore, He mentioned those places to remind them of the miracles that occurred during those years. The Jewish people were miraculously sustained by the *mon* and the water well of Miriam. The clouds of glory miraculously protected them from all dangers. Remembering and reviewing these wondrous events helped them to remember and have faith in Hashem, the One who cared for them."

"Wow, Avi. I never realized the significance of those travels.

Can I share with you something that I just thought of?"

"Sure, Chaim."

"We can do this very same thing in our own lives. As we look back, we can sometimes piece together events and see Hashem's hand guiding us along the way. Something may have looked very bad at the time it happened. A few years later, when we have time to look back and reflect, we see that the event was not bad at all, but a step on the way to something very good. Reviewing these acts of kindness that Hashem has done for us in our lives will strengthen our own faith in Him."

"Chaim, this piece of wisdom is a major stop on the road map of my life. I don't need to look back to see how important it is. You have given me the key to seeing things in perspective. Stop. Think. Put things together. See the big picture."

Simcha's Brain Teaser

Mr. and Mrs. Kaplan had five sons. Each son had one sister. How many children did the Kaplans have?

For the answer, turn to the back of the book.

Devarim

Parashas Devarim

Cosmic Message

Avi. Avi."

"Oh. Hello Chaim. Shalom. How are you?"

"Fine. Did you hear me calling you?"

"I was so absorbed in the science fiction story that I am reading that I didn't hear you."

"Can I read it?"

"Sure, Chaim. Here it is."

One cold, clear, winter evening in the observatory, high atop a mountain in northern Washington...

"Come quickly, Dr. Benson. Look at this!"

Dr. Benson rushes from the other end of the deserted laboratory to join his colleague, Dr. Rosen, in front of the radio-telescope screen.

"Do you see this on the screen?"

Dr. Benson's eyes open wide. "It looks like a message coming in."

"Exactly."

"Who could be transmitting this message?"

"We must investigate. Read me the coordinates of the radio telescope."

"39° north, 147° east."

"That cannot be."

"Why not?"

"The nearest star in that quadrant is 3300 light years away. That means that the message that we are receiving has been traveling at the speed of light for 3300 years."

"Do you mean that the senders of this message began transmission 3300 years ago? They must all be long gone by now. Nevertheless, their message is reaching us today."

Words slowly form and fill the screen. The two scientists are in awe of what they are seeing.

"Dr. Benson, this will make international news headlines. A communication from the distant past. A message launched across 3300 years of history..."

"Chaim. Chaim."

"Yes, Avi. I'm sorry. I was very absorbed in the story. A message from 3300 years ago! You know, Avi, the story has some truth to it."

"Really Chaim? In what way?"

"The first verse in the Book of Devarim states, 'These are the words that Moshe spoke to all of Israel...' Moshe gathered the Jewish people together in the desert, shortly before their entrance to Eretz Yisrael. It was there that he delivered his final message to the Jewish people before he passed on from this world. Rav Chaim ben Atar, the great *rav* who lived about 250 years ago, wrote a commentary on the Torah entitled *Ohr HaChaim.*

There he explains why the expression 'all Israel' was used instead of just stating 'Israel.' Moshe was not speaking only to those Jews present in the desert at that time. Rather he was addressing all of the Jews of all future generations. These words of Torah that he was about to convey to them were timeless.

"There are no other words in existence that can inspire and guide a people throughout history like the Torah. So you see, Avi, every time that we read and learn the Torah, we are receiving a message that began transmission 3300 years ago, and is still going strong today."

"What a cosmic experience. If people realized this, they would be standing in lines from here to Cincinnati to read the message."

"Avi, let's see what we can do to help people realize the timeless value of the Torah."

"I'm with you, cosmic buddy. Let's blast off!"

Simcha's Brain Teaser

What is the closest relation that your father's sister's sister-in-law could be to you?

For the answer, turn to the back of the book.

Is More Really Better?

How did you do on the test, Avi?"

"I got an 80, Chaim."

"That's good."

"What did you get Chaim?"

"Eighty-five."

"That's better than 80."

"That's right, more is better."

A short time later...

"Come, Yitzi, let's trade baseball cards. I have over one hundred cards in my collection."

"One hundred cards. That's nothing! I have 250 cards."

"Wow, Yitzi. Your collection is better than mine. You have more cards."

"That's right! More is better!"

A short time later...

"What flavor ice cream did you get, Avi?"

"Chocolate. What did you get, Menachem?"

"I got two dips. Mocha and vanilla."

"Two dips! You got more ice cream than I did. Your cone is better than mine."

"That's right, more is better."

A short time later Avi is walking along thinking to himself...

"More is better. More is better. More is better. I have been hearing that expression quite a bit. The more you have of something, the better off you are. Hmmm. I have an idea."

Avi arrives home.

"Daddy! I'm home!"

"Avi! Great to see you! How was your day?"

"Great, Daddy! I really learned a lot today."

"What did you learn, Avi?"

"One of the things I learned is that 'more is better.' The more you have of something, the better off you are. I have a brainstorm."

"Great! Let's hear it!"

"How many tzitzis are on your tallis?"

"Four."

"Let's add a fifth one. After all, more is better."

"Hmmm."

"I have another idea, Daddy."

"Yes, Avi."

"Next Sukkos, instead of waving four types of plants — esrog, lulav, hadasim, and aravos — let's add a fifth type. After all, more is better."

"Hmmm. Avi, what you are saying is not exactly true."

"What do you mean, Daddy?"

"It may be true that more is better when it comes to test scores and baseball card collections, but mitzvos are different. The Torah gives us precise instructions how to perform a mitzvah; it tells us exactly how much of each component to use."

"How do you know that, Daddy?"

"It is in this week's *parashah*, Avi. Moshe Rabbeinu is speaking to the Jewish people just before they are about to enter Eretz Yisrael after their forty years in the desert. He tells them (Devarim 4:2), 'You shall not add to the word that I command you, nor shall you subtract from it...' Rashi explains that we are cautioned against doing exactly what you suggested, Avi — having five tzitzis instead of four, or adding a fifth plant to the *arba minim*. So you see, when it comes to mitzvos, more is not necessarily better. Mitzvos are a precise science. The instructions must be followed very carefully."

"It's like driving a car, Daddy. You can't drive too fast or too slow."

"Exactly, Avi."

"Or like eating dinner. If you eat too little, you won't have enough energy. And if you eat too much, you will be sick."

"You've really got the hang of it."

"I'm learning exactly how to understand the exactness of a mitzvah."

"Exactly!"

Simcha's Brain Teaser

Ninety-seven students participate in a Torah knowledge contest. The champion is chosen by the standard elimination schedule. That is, the 97 students are divided into pairs, and each student competes against the other. After a student is eliminated from each pair, the winners are again divided into pairs, etc. How many pair eliminations must be played to determine a champion?

For the answer, turn to the back of the book.

Parashas Eikev

It Only Takes One

I *have so much to do. How will I ever manage?*

"How are you Avi?"

"I'm feeling swamped, Chaim."

"Really? Why?"

"I have so much to do. I don't know how I will ever manage."

"Come, Avi. Let me help you. Let's make a list and tackle your projects one by one."

"List? List? I already have a list. It hasn't helped me."

"Let me see your list, Avi. Maybe I can help you."

"Look in the Torah and you will see my list, Chaim."

"What are you talking about, Avi?"

"My list is the list of mitzvos in the Torah — 613 mitzvos. So many mitzvos. So much to do. How will I ever manage to do them all?"

"You are feeling overwhelmed by the sheer number of mitzvos in the Torah, Avi?"

"That's right, Chaim."

"Hmmm. Let me think about this a minute. I think there is a verse in this week's *parashah* that will be very encouraging to you."

"Please tell me. What is it?"

"Chapter 8, verse 1. 'All the mitzvah which I command you (singular) today, guard it in order to perform it...' "

"Aren't you making a mistake in grammar, Chaim? The verse should read, 'All the *mitzvos* which I command *you* (plural)...' "

"Very perceptive of you, Avi. Rav Shlomo Efraim from Lontshetz, who is known by the name of his classic commentary on the Torah, the *Kli Yakar,* asks the same question. Why does the verse use the word 'mitzvah' in the singular instead of the plural form? Why does the verse also use the word 'you' in the singular instead of the plural form? After all, Moshe was speaking to the entire Jewish nation."

"Wow. I feel better already, Chaim. I asked the same question that the Kli Yakar asked. That means that I have my thinking cap on."

"His answer will make you feel even better, Avi. He explains that the word 'you' is written in the singular to teach us that one person can change the entire world."

"How?"

"If he is making mistakes in his mitzvah observance, he need only correct those mistakes. That will exert a powerful enough influence to change the whole world."

"Wow. What about the other part of the verse?"

"The word 'mitzvah' is written in the singular to teach us that if a person does just one mitzvah properly, he will merit eternal life."

"I never realized that, Chaim."

"You are right, Avi. There are many mitzvos to perform. Sometimes it can seem like an impossible task. We have to take them one at a time. But just think about the words of the Kli Yakar. One person can change the whole world. One mitzvah can change your whole life. It only takes one."

"Chaim, thank you so much. I don't feel overwhelmed anymore. I just have to keep repeating it to myself."

"Repeating what, Avi?"

" 'It only takes one.' "

Simcha's Brain Teaser

Devora can walk at 2 mph going up a mountain. Going down the same trail, she can walk at 6 mph. If she spends no time at the top, what will be Devora's average speed for the whole hike?

For the answer, turn to the back of the book.

Parashas Re'eh

Repetition

"Did you figure out the answer to the teacher's question yet, Chaim?"

"Which question are you referring to, Avi?"

"The one about charity."

"Hmmm. I don't remember the question so clearly, Avi. Could you remind me what he said?"

"Sure. Imagine that you had one hundred dollars to give to charity. Is it better to give the entire sum to one poor person, or give one dollar each to one hundred poor people?"

"Now I remember the question. Let's think about this a minute. If you give to one hundred poor people, you are helping one hundred people. That's a lot better than helping just one person."

"That's true, Chaim, but how much are you really helping each person? One dollar isn't very much. On the other hand, if you give the whole one hundred dollars to one poor person, you are really giving him a big helping hand."

"You have a good point, Avi. So do I. Each answer has its advantage and disadvantage."

"The Chafetz Chaim has a different angle on this question.

He focuses on what is better for the giver of the charity, not the receiver. If you look in this week's *parashah* you will see that the Torah repeats the word 'give' twice when instructing us to give charity to the poor (Devarim 15:10). Rashi comments that the Torah repeats the word to teach us that as long as the poor remain needy we must give to them. Even one hundred times."

"I'm not following you, Avi. What difference does it make to the giver how many times he gives? It's the same amount of money in either case."

"That's true, Chaim. However, imagine yourself as the giver. A man comes to you to ask for charity. You give to him. He returns the next day. You give again. This continues for a week. Then another week. And another week. After a while you begin to think, 'Can't this man get a job? Why does he keep coming back to me?' However, the Torah instructs you to give. Therefore, you keep giving.

"Each time that you give, it gets a little easier. You take one more step towards overcoming your inclination to ignore the poor person. After one hundred times, the giving becomes second nature to you. You have become a generous person. You would never accomplish this by writing one check for one hundred dollars. One hundred acts of giving make a much bigger impression upon a person than a single moment of generosity."

"I see, Avi. It's like exercise in a way. Daily training is much more beneficial to you than one massive workout."

"Now you're getting the hang of it, Chaim. The Torah wants you to develop your 'giving' muscles. Therefore, you have to exercise them regularly."

"You've changed my whole attitude towards charity, Avi.

Each person that comes asking for charity is another opportunity for me to get some exercise."

"Chaim, you're really getting into shape. Keep up the repetitions!"

Simcha's Brain Teaser

If some coffee is "97 percent caffeine-free," how many cups of it would one have to drink to get the amount of caffeine in a cup of regular coffee?

For the answer, turn to the back of the book.

The Right Thing

Our friend Avi is sitting in the classroom, taking a science test, thinking to himself, *Boy, this test sure is hard. I thought that I studied well, but some things I don't remember and others I just don't understand.*

He reads the next two questions on the test.

"How far away is the moon from the earth?"

"How often does the moon circle the earth?"

I remember studying that, but I just can't remember the answers. Oy vey. I studied so much and I'm not going to do well on this test. I'll be so embarrassed. Mommy and Daddy will be upset with me. What am I going to do?

Suddenly, Avi comes up with an idea.

I know what I'll do. In my pocket are the index cards with my study notes written on them. I will ask the teacher to be excused for a minute. When I am outside the classroom, I can take the cards out of my pocket and find the answers! No one will ever know.

"Excuse me, Mr. Warfield, may I please be excused?"

"Of course, Avi."

Once outside, Avi takes the cards out of his pocket. Much to his surprise, he finds his notes from *parashas hashavua* class instead of science class.

He reads the first card. " '*Tzedek tzedek tirdof* — You shall pursue righteousness' (Devarim 16:20). The Torah commands us to be just and fair in all of our deeds."

Avi reads the words over and over again. "The Torah commands us to be just and fair in all of our deeds. Just and fair in all of our deeds."

He thinks to himself, *What is unfair about looking at my notes? After all, I did study the material. I just can't remember a couple of answers. Do I have to suffer a bad grade just for that? And whom am I hurting? No one will suffer if I get a good grade. My parents will be very happy and proud of me. What's wrong with looking at my notes?*

Avi is about to look at his science notes. He stops a moment and continues thinking.

Looking at notes is against the rules. The teachers have good reasons for making the rules. Some of the reasons we understand. If we were allowed to look at notes, no one would study. Then no one would learn anything. But I already studied and learned, so why can't I look at the notes? Because it is against the rules. If I break the rules, I will corrupt the system. Worse than that, I will corrupt myself. It was no accident that I pulled out the index card with parashas hashavua written on it. "Tzedek tzedek tirdof." We must be righteous and just in all of our deeds.

Avi returns to the test without looking at his notes.

I guess I'll answer the questions that I know and the others leave blank. Wait a minute! I just remembered something! The moon is 240,000 miles from the earth! The moon circles the earth once every 29½ days. Baruch Hashem!

Avi happily thinks to himself, *I've learned a big lesson from all of this. I must always do the right thing. No matter how easy and harmless it seems to break the rules, breaking the rules is wrong to do. And we have to do...the right thing.*

Simcha's Brain Teaser

What goes around the world and sits in one corner?

For the answer, turn to the back of the book.

Union Shop

"Chaim, what did you learn about in history class today?"

"Labor unions, Avi."

"Really? That sounds fascinating. What did the teacher say?"

"He told us that about one hundred years ago, many factories were referred to as 'sweatshops.' "

"Why was that, Chaim?"

"Working conditions were very poor. The workers had long hours without breaks, the wages were very low, and the work was dangerous. The workers were very dissatisfied."

"What did they do about it?"

"They banded together and formed labor unions. The unions fought for normal working conditions and went on strike if their demands were not met."

"Sounds like a good thing."

"It was for the most part, Avi. However, the unions realized that they had power, and in certain instances they abused that power, taking advantage of the owners. It was a struggle, with each side trying to gain the upper hand."

"So, let me see if I got this right, Chaim. The factory owners took advantage of the workers. When the workers finally got power, they took advantage of the factory owners."

"That's it, Avi."

"That would never happen if everyone followed the Torah's laws about employer-employee relationships."

"Really, Avi? I never knew such a thing existed."

"Certainly, Chaim. This week's *parashah, Ki Seitzei,* deals with bosses and workers."

"What does it say?"

"Imagine that you owned an orchard, Chaim, and you hired workers to pick your fruit. You must allow those workers to eat some of the fruit when they are going between the rows of trees. The *Sefer HaChinuch,* a *sefer* written by one of the great Rabbis almost one thousand years ago, explains the following: A boss should be kind and generous to his workers. This will allow Hashem to bestow all of His blessings upon him. An oppressive and overbearing boss exhibits very bad qualities. Only bad will come to him."

"You know, Avi, that reminds me of something that our Gemara rebbe once taught us. One who is serving the food at a meal must be allowed to eat before he serves. It would be cruel to make him serve while he is hungry."

"Exactly the point, Chaim. Now we have addressed half of the problem — the boss's obligation to the worker. What about the worker's obligation to the boss? The very next mitzvah in the Torah commands the worker who is picking the fruit to eat only what he needs. He should not get carried away and assume that since the owner must allow him to eat, he is also allowed to take some home for his family to eat. That would be stealing. He is not allowed to take advantage of the owner. He can only eat what he needs."

"What wisdom the Torah teaches, Avi! The boss must be concerned about the worker, and the worker must be considerate of the boss. Each one is concerned for the other. If the 'sweat-shop' bosses and workers had followed the Torah, they could have avoided all of those problems."

"That is why Shlomo HaMelech, the wisest of all men, wrote about the Torah, 'Its ways are pleasant and all of its paths are peaceful' (Mishlei 3:17)."

Simcha's Brain Teaser

The owner of the local bank found a $50 bill lying in the gutter. He picked it up and made a note of its serial number. Later that day his wife mentioned that they owed the butcher $50, so the banker used the bill he'd found to settle up with the butcher. The butcher used it to pay a farmer; the farmer in turn used it pay his feedstock supplier; and the feedstock supplier used it to pay his laundry bill. The laundryman used it to pay off his $50 overdraft at the local bank. The banker recognized the bill as being the one he had found in the gutter, but also noticed, on closer examination, that it was a fake. By now, it had been used to settle $250 worth of debts. What was lost?

For the answer, turn to the back of the book.

More than a Trillion Gigabytes

Hi, Avi, where are you going?"

"I'm on my way to the computer store, Chaim. Do you want to come?"

"Sure! What are you going to do there?"

"I'm going to buy a new hard drive for my computer."

"What's the matter with your old one? Is it getting soft?"

"Don't be silly, Chaim. Hard drives don't get soft; they just get filled up."

"Is yours filled up already? I remember when you bought it, just a few months ago."

"That's right, Chaim. However, the computer programs and files that I am storing on my hard drive are getting bigger and bigger all the time. They take up more and more space. Now I have no space left and I need a new, bigger hard drive. This old one just cannot hold any more information."

"Wow! I just thought of a great idea, Avi. Let's invent a hard drive that gets bigger as you put more and more information on it. You will never have to buy a new hard drive. The old one will just keep expanding and expanding."

"Chaim, that's a great idea, but we all know that it is impossible. It is against the laws of physics. The more you fill something up, the less space you have left."

"I guess you're right, Avi. It was a good thought."

"But wait, Chaim, there is something that gets bigger the more you fill it."

"You just said it was impossible."

"That's true, but I was only thinking about man-made containers. They are always limited in size. However, when Hashem makes a container, He does a much better job than we do."

"What are you talking about, Avi?"

"This week's *parashah*, Chaim. The verse begins, 'If you will listen to the voice of Hashem...' (Devarim 28:1). The word 'listen' is repeated twice."

"Why would the Torah repeat a word twice? We know that the Torah does not waste even one single word."

"The Torah is teaching us something. Our Sages explain that

the word 'listen' is referring to listening to words of Torah and learning them. The word 'listen' is repeated twice to teach us that the more you listen, the more you are able to listen. The more you learn, the more you are able to learn. There is no way to 'fill up' your brain cells. You can never 'use up' all of your memory. Quite the opposite. The more you use your brain, the better it works. The more you exercise your memory, the more you are able to remember."

"You know, Avi, we are all amazed when we see the intricate workings of a computer. But it is nothing but a simple toy compared to the human brain."

"Exactly my point, Chaim. Let's make a simple calculation. How many pages are contained in all of the volumes of the Talmud? About 2700. Each page is very big with very small print — there are hundreds of words on each one. Each line is packed with many different ideas and pieces of information. These ideas are all interrelated in very complicated patterns and relationships. There must be millions of ideas and relationships in the volumes and volumes of Talmud."

"Very true, Avi."

"The preeminent sage of our time, Rav Moshe Feinstein, of blessed memory, learned the entire Talmud at least 202 times. He committed it to memory. He also knew the ten-volume code of Torah law known as the *Shulchan Aruch.* Can you imagine how much he knew? Yet his memory kept expanding to learn more and more Torah. The 'hard drive' that Hashem put into our heads is better than any we can buy in the computer store. However, there is one condition. We have to use it. It only grows if we use it."

"Avi, I hope you don't mind if I don't walk you home from

the computer store. I want to be on time for my learning session. I have lots and lots of Torah to learn. I still have trillions and trillions of megabytes left on my drive."

Simcha's Brain Teaser

You are given ten baskets. Nine of the baskets have ten balls weighing 10 pounds per ball, however one basket has ten balls weighing 9 pounds each. All the balls and baskets are identical in appearance. You are asked to determine which basket contains the 9-pound balls. You have a suitable scale, but may only take a single measurement. No other measurements may be taken (like trying to determine by hand). You may remove balls from the baskets but may still only take one measurement.

For the answer, turn to the back of the book.

Parashas Nitzavim

We're All in the Same Boat

W hat a wonderful boat ride, Avi. Smell the salt air. Look at
the beautiful view. The gentle ocean breeze and the rock-
ing of the boat are so calming."

"Chaim, I'm glad you told me about this. It was a great idea.
It's so quiet out here."

Suddenly the noise of an electric power tool shatters the
calm.

Zzzzzzzzzzzzzzzzzz.

"What's that noise, Avi?"

"I don't know, Chaim. It sounded like an electric drill or saw."

Zzzzzzzzzzzzzzzzzz.

"There it is again. It's coming from over there, farther back
on the boat. Let's go see what it is."

The two boys go back to investigate and see a very strange sight.
Crouching under one of the seats is a man holding a power drill. He is
drilling a hole under his seat through the bottom of the boat.

"Avi, can you believe it? That man is drilling a hole in the
bottom of the boat! This whole boat will sink and we'll have to
swim back to shore. This is dangerous business. We had better
tell the captain."

"Wait a minute, Chaim. Let's talk to the man first. He probably doesn't realize what he is doing. When we tell him, I'm sure he will stop. Excuse me, sir."

"Yes. What do you want?"

"I just wanted to point something out to you. You probably don't realize that if you continue drilling like that, you will put a hole in the bottom of the boat."

"Listen, young man, I know exactly what I am doing. What I do under my own seat is of no concern to you. I paid full fare for this seat, and it is mine for the duration of this trip. You have no right to tell me what I can or cannot do under my seat. Now leave me alone."

"You're right, Avi, let's go to the captain."

The boys run to the captain and report the man. His drilling is stopped before he can put a hole in the boat.

"Boys, we don't know how to thank you. You saved the whole boat. I'm going to see to it that you get free passes on this boat ride whenever you want. We owe you a real debt of gratitude. That man was very strange. How could he think that because he bought a seat, he has the right to drill a hole under it? Didn't he feel any connection or responsibility to the other passengers?"

"Mr. Captain, sir, it's funny you should bring that up. We were just learning about that in school this week."

"Really? What class teaches you about boat passengers?"

"Our class on the weekly Torah portion. Three thousand two hundred and seventy years ago, our ancestors were about to enter the Land of Israel. One of the last things they did before entering the land was to form a pact pledging mutual responsibility to one another. Every Jew became responsible for every member of the Jewish people. The deeds of each person would affect all of the others."

"What does that have to do with the boat passengers?"

"To put it figuratively, since that time the Jewish people have all been in the same boat together. When one of us does something good, we all benefit. On the other hand, if any one of us does something wrong, we all suffer. If any member of our nation violates the Sabbath or eats non-kosher food, he is not only hurting himself, he is hurting the Jewish people as a whole. He might think that observing the mitzvos are his own private business. They are not. They are everyone's business. Just like the man on the boat. We would all suffer from his foolish deed."

"Boys, I truly admire you and your people. Communal responsibility is a very important thing. People who bind together can accomplish great things. Much more than separate individuals."

"Mr. Captain, sir, we have accomplished great things. The next time we take this boat ride, we can tell you all about our amazing 3800 year history."

"Boys, it will be my pleasure. You can sit up in the main cabin with me. People who took the responsibility to save the boat deserve the best seats. I want to hear all about the 3800 year boat ride of the Jewish people."

Simcha's Brain Teaser

A ship is at anchor. Over the side hangs a rope ladder with rungs a foot apart. The tide rises at a rate of 8 inches per hour. At the end of six hours, how much of the rope ladder will remain above water, assuming that 8 feet were above the water when the tide began to rise?

For the answer, turn to the back of the book.